GOD AT WORK
in
Glassford, Chapelton and Central Africa

GOD AT WORK

in

Glassford, Chapelton and Central Africa

(A story of God at work in two villages in Lanarkshire and its far-reaching results)

By

Jack Murdoch

JOHN RITCHIE LTD
CHRISTIAN PUBLICATIONS

40 Beansburn, Kilmarnock, Scotland

ISBN-13: 978 1 907731 24 2

Copyright © 2010 by John Ritchie Ltd.
40 Beansburn, Kilmarnock, Scotland

www.ritchiechristianmedia.co.uk

Typeset by John Ritchie Ltd., Kilmarnock
Printed by Bell & Bain Ltd., Glasgow

Contents

Introduction

I first became interested in writing this book through my contacts with Martha and David Kinnaird of Chapelton, following on my involvement with them, at a critical final stage of their children's work in Chapelton village.

The Kinnaird's, with other helpers, have been involved, particularly in their work among Chapelton children for thirty eight years. They still live in the village, as I write. Many of the villagers and their children will have happy memories of this work. Some are now adults, while others have moved on to live elsewhere.

Also, around fifty years ago, through my previous connections with Martha's father, in Glassford, I had become aware of a book, which he greatly prized and which even then, had been out of print for many years. On his decease, the book was passed on to David and Martha. They kindly loaned me it so that I could write this book.

This red, hard-backed book goes back to the nineteenth century, and tells the story of the conversion, during the spiritual revival of 1859, of the Chapelton village publican, whose premises occupied a focal point- which can still be seen - at the centre of the old part of the village. It also records, at greater length, the story of his daughter, Jeanie Gilchrist. Jeanie became the first Scottish lady missionary to accompany the well-known missionary Fred Stanley Arnot to Central Africa, sixteen years after David Livingstone died among the swamps of East Central Africa.

It was the children's work of David and Martha; the story of the publican's conversion and the missionary work of his daughter, Jeanie, which prompted me to write the major part of this book about God at work, in Chapelton, leading in Jeanie's case to her missionary activities in Central Africa. This part of the book begins in 1859 and ends almost 150 years later in 2004.

I make no claim to cover all aspects of God's work in Chapelton or in Central Africa, during those years, but instead I have concentrated on those events, which, because of my background, have been of particular interest to me.

** **

In the process of producing the book, I decided to include other stories which greatly interested me, as I grew up in Glassford village, near Chapelton, in the mid -1930's and early 1940's.

Our family lived upstairs in a tenement block, shared by three other families. The Parkers lived opposite us, separated by a stone landing and we shared a basic toilet at the bottom of a short enclosed stairway: in winter, the water was often frozen over! I remember the street lights being turned on for the first time.

The winters were often severe, like the exceptional one just experienced in 2009/2010 and sometimes the local primary school was closed for days, until some workmen managed to clear the way through deep snowdrifts, which blocked the school entrance.

There were fewer cars then, and a visit to the sea side in Ayr, on a warm summer day, was a real treat. TV wasn't yet invented, "*Tammy Troot*" was the radio programme, I liked most. Telephone communication was mainly through the local, public telephone box: mobile phones, personal computers, laptops and iPods did not exist. There was no local library.

The local farm, tucked on to the end of the village, was a key attraction. I remember on one occasion, the bull broke loose causing a "bull-run" up the village street: those of us who happened to be there at the time, dived for safety into one of the surprised villagers' cottages, which lined one side of the street, while a farm worker chased the bull with a pitch-fork. Tractors had not yet been introduced, so the local farm (now sold and given over to housing), had two strong Clydesdale work horses. In early autumn, after we helped farmer "Jock" Davidson "build his hayricks, it was fun to sit on the empty, flat *"rucklifter,"* behind one of those powerful horses, as we headed for the field to help bring the hay into his barn.

We roamed the countryside and while there, my curiosity was aroused by stories, which I heard, largely connected with the local area's *early history:* there was some evidence to support them, but no means to substantiate them. I determined that one day I would investigate and these are my findings: I hope you will find them interesting.

So, the first part of the book is about early activities in Glassford and Chapelton.

**

Chapelton and Glassford (known locally as "the Glessart") were part of Glassford Parish, until 1876, and the two countryside villages are located in Lanarkshire, in lowland Scotland, lying to the south east of the busy central belt, which surrounds the major city of Glasgow. They are separated by the A723 road, from Strathaven to Hamilton; Chapelton being on the west and **Glassford** some 3 miles south-east of Chapelton.

The word *Chapelton* defines the origin of the village; being derived from an ancient place of worship or *chapel,* which was fenced in for this purpose-*ton* or *toun.* It was given to distinguish it from pagan worship of the time.

**

With only one exception, the stories I heard have a *religious* connection and in their own way, point to or add their own contribution to my story of, "God at work" in this area.

But let me now deal with the *rumour* I heard, which has no religious connection but which, I am sure, you will find interesting.

The story, circulating in Glassford during the Second World War, which ended in 1945, was that an underground tunnel had been secretly built, by the army, from Hallhill to Muirburn, close to the river Avon, some $1\frac{1}{2}$ miles away from Hallhill. As I remember it, there was a substantial soft fruit farm at Muirburn just after the war, and, in summer, we would earn a few pence picking strawberries and gooseberries there, which made a small addition to our meagre family income. Like other young villagers, I first learned to swim in the *"big or wee Kentucky,"* close to the Avon Bridge, just below the Muirburn mansion.

The most likely reason for the rumour is that the villagers were aware of some event of historical significance associated with Hallhill, but were not sure what it was. (Hallhill lies on the left hand side of the road leading from the village to the graveyard.) They also knew that something strange was going on, at Muirburn, during the war, as it had been closed to the public. Putting two and two together - and making five - the rumour circulated that the Army had built a tunnel from Hallhill to Muirburn and that some secret activities were going on!

The facts are somewhat different. At Hallhill, a castle had been built, facing the mansion house there, centuries ago, and its existence as a ruin had been reported as early as 1540. This ruin was in the form of an arch structure, which could house up to one hundred soldiers and was finally demolished, in 1828.

So what was going on at Muirburn during the Second World War?

The land owners, the Alstons,(there is a street in Glassford called *Alston Street* and my mother was brought up there) had died before the First World War and the Mansion they had built was sold to the Lanarkshire Burgh to be a Sanatorium. The idea was not taken up and the building fell into disrepair. During the war, the Ministry of Defence used it as a testing site for new explosives (TNT) and the house was reduced to rubble.

When the war ended, the remaining soft fruit garden must have been taken over by a new tenant or owner, hence the reason we youngsters were hired to help with the fruit picking.

**

PART ONE
Early activities in Glassford and Chapelton

ANCIENT DRUIDS

While out in the countryside, near Avonholm, Glassford, my pal, James Leishman, pointed to two stones on the grass path leading from Avonholm to the Glassford graveyard and said: "These are Druid stones!"

His identification of the stones was incorrect, but he made me aware, of the possibility of evidence of ancient Druid activities in the area: but no one seemed to know where the Druid stones were.

Later, I learned that they were in a wooded area, not far from where he had pointed to the other stones that day. Locals referred to the area where the Druid Stones were as, "*The Dogs' Graveyard.*"

It was not, in fact, simply a dogs' graveyard, but was the final resting place of, the Struthers of Avonholm". They chose to be buried there, next to the three large, unshaped Druid Stones, in a small, fenced, burial ground, along with their three dogs. The flat stones mark the burial place of the dogs and the tabled stones theirs.

When new houses were built in Glassford after the Second World War, one of the streets was named Druid Street – and the Leishman family lived there.

As my initial interest in writing this book concerned events in Chapelton, I discovered that it too had claims to a Druid Stone: this stone existed up until 1940, in the field, on the opposite side of the public road from Shawton House.

So what is the case for the Druids: did they really exist and if so, who were they?

One thing is certain, they did not advance my main theme of *God at work* but, perhaps they can point to Someone who did!

**

Not a great deal is known about the ancient Druids.

They were part of an ancient people collectively known as the Celts, who inhabited Ireland, Britain and a substantial area of North Western Europe, from around 1200BC to 200AD. By the time the Romans invaded Britain, the people there had formed themselves into large tribal groups able to defend themselves from rival tribes and the invading forces, using horses and iron chariots.

The Celts, like many other primitive societies, had no written language, so what we know about them and the Druids comes mainly from the *Greek and Roman writers*, who came into direct contact with them and from archaeological excavations.

The Celtic people occupied a wide geographical area, and cultures and values differed according to their locality. Ireland was never occupied by the Romans and although the Romans invaded **Scotland** in AD81, by AD 122, they had withdrawn from their occupation of lowland and central Scotland, behind the protection of *Hadrian's Wall*, which they built, as a defence from the north, across Britain, roughly marking the boundary between Scotland and England.

The Romans did make further attempts to occupy Scotland, occupying the lowlands, and building the *Antonine Wall*, in AD 143, stretching across Scotland from the west coast to the Firth of Forth in the east. But, this they later abandoned and by AD 160, they finally retreated, again behind the protection of Hadrian's Wall. Remains of part of these walls can still be seen today.

As the contacts of the Romans with the Celtic tribes is one of the major sources of information about the Druids, and as their contacts with the Scottish Druids were extremely limited, what we can deduce about our local Druids is scant, other than through our knowledge of them in the wider Celtic world.

The Roman writers, including Julius Caesar, following his military campaigns, wrote about the Druids and it was Roman laws directed against the Druids, which led to their demise throughout the Roman Empire. *Tacitus*, writing about the British Druids, stated that by AD 61, the Druids had been stamped out. This could hardly have been the case, with those in Glassford and Chapelton, as the Romans did not invade Scotland until AD 81, as I mentioned earlier. Perhaps our local Druids continued to function for some years later.

From the above-mentioned sources and later archaeological finds, a reasonable picture of the Druids can be constructed.

They were part of a learned and priestly class, including bards and seers, who exercised an important role in the Celtic community.

Since they had no written language, one of their key tasks was to select and train suitable successors, who would be able to memorise and pass on to future generations, the oral traditions concerning the beliefs and ceremonies and laws and customs of their local culture.

The name, "Druid" was coined by those early writers. It appears to have been derived from the Greek word for an oak tree (*Drus*), taken, it is thought, from the Druid practice of meeting in cleared, deciduous forest areas to carry out their teaching and engage in their religious ceremonies.

The writers, I referred to earlier, describe these ceremonies; including the ritual cutting down of *mistletoe* branches from an oak tree; a Druid priest officiating at religious ceremonies, while dressed in a white robe, and the sacrifice of two white bulls. *Tacitus* refers to the British Druids, 'covering the altars with the blood of their captives and consulting their deities through human entrails.'

Their worship ceremonies involved *human sacrifices* to their gods.

The Druids possessed astronomical skills from which they were able to work out their own special 'holy days' and calendars. In this, they were akin to the *magi* or wise men from the East, referred to in the Bible, who followed the *Star* to find the child Jesus and present to Him their gifts. One of the Druids special days, we now recognise as *Hallo'een* and our Christmas celebrations had their origin in these pagan, winter festivals.

Archaeological findings have revealed that the Celts had a belief in immortality: they believed that life after death was a continuation of their present life, in an immaterial body and made provision for this in the articles they buried with their dead.

The Druid influence in the Celtic community, at large was brought to an end by the Romans, who passed and enforced laws forbidding the Barbaric practices associated with *human sacrifice*. It was a case of: *"Don't do as I do but do as I tell you!"*, as the Romans continued to commit atrocities, including throwing Christians to the lions in their arenas.

Centuries after Druid activities had ceased, attempts were made, to trace the Druid origins back to the patriarchs in the Bible. A link was made with Jacob, Abraham's grand-son, whose activities were sometimes associated with *oak trees,* and who also *erected pillars of stone* – and didn't Abraham, on one very special occasion, offer up his own son as a *human sacrifice*? But there is no such link.

Some modern-day "Druids" claim to be descendants of those earlier British Druids. On special Druid holy days, they gathered round the *Stonehenge, Standing Stones,* in England. There, dressed in white robes, they perform their ceremonial rituals – without, of course, involving human sacrifice!

Around Britain, there are a number of sites with Standing Stones, which brings me back to the Druid Stones in Glassford and Chapelton, which I referred to earlier.

Clearly the belief that these stones had a connection with the Druids goes back a long time. Rev. William T. Stewart in his excellent book, *"Glasford – the Kirk and the Kingdom"*, mentions a long-standing connection between the three "Druid "stones in Glassford and an ancient road, which terminated in what, is now, *"Threestanes Road"* in Strathaven.

As I was researching the early history of religious activities in the area, I became aware of Bill's book, published in September 1988. (His spelling of the village's name is an alternative earlier spelling).

I attended the *Glasford Kirk*, with my mother and her children in my youth (indeed, I once sang, a solo verse, as part of a small children's choir in, *"The holly and the ivy"* – how tolerant congregations were in those days!).

My mother and Aunt Jenny were members of the *Glasford Kirk* and are mentioned in Bill's book. I was given a loan of the book, by a near neighbour, Robert Parker. It was Robert and his parents who shared the same upstairs section, across the landing, of the tenement building in which our families lived, in Glassford, more than half-a-century ago! The book was gifted to his mother, Janet Parker, by its author Bill Stewart as a thank-you gift for the information she had provided. After all those years, it is remarkable that Robert and his wife live, only three houses away!

If you can obtain a copy of Bill Stewart's book, his comments on the Druids and other local history of the Glassford area are well worth reading: his sense of humour throughout the book makes for easy reading.

He has a chapter on the "Standing Stones" (in the "*dogs' graveyard*", which I mentioned earlier) and has kindly agreed to me reproducing this animating excerpt:

"How stirring, how romantic to think of Glasford men and women, two or three thousand years ago, gathering round these ancient stones to watch the white-clad priests perform the annual rituals, placating the gods for the blessing of all.

How stirring! How romantic! But was it?

Stirring yes! Not so romantic for the chosen victim of the sacrifice, dragged struggling and screaming to the altar, where the Druid priest waited, with sharpened knife, to slit his throat and to sprinkle his blood on the stones or the nearby yew, at the midnight on the feast of Samain, the high point in the Druids' year". What a vivid piece of writing!

I leave you to make up your own mind on the significance of these "Druid" stones.

As an appropriate ending to this excursion on the Druids, Bill's ending to this section of his book is in keeping with my theme, "God at work":

"But by now a stronger force than Rome had come to challenge Druid power. This force was born in Bethlehem of Judea, in the days of Herod the King."

An inscription by George Henry Law, Bishop of Bath and Wells in the 19th Century conveys the same message: it bears the words:

*Here once where druids trod in times of yore
And stained their altars with a victim's gore,
Here now the Christian ransomed from above,
Adores a God of mercy and of love.*

* *

19

COVENANTERS

Personal recollections

A Covenanter's Monument occupies a prominent position on the roadside of the older section of the Glassford graveyard. What was it about graveyards - dogs and human - that seemed to fascinate me so much?

My curiosity was provoked by the words, just about legible, carved on this monument – *If a hard fate demands or claims a tear, stay gentle passenger and shed it here.* Who were the Covenanters and what was the story behind these words?

That early curiosity was further stirred by the choice of *Old Mortality, by Sir Walter Scott,* for my university Higher English exam: an exciting, historical fiction, set in 1679, based on the Covenanters' struggles in Lanarkshire, at that time.

If that were not enough to make me investigate, more was to follow. Having had a banking background, (not a plus point perhaps, in the current Credit Crunch climate!) when I reached the age for National Service, taking the easy way out, I opted for the army *Pay Corps.* The powers that be, assigned me instead to the then lowland regiment, the *Cameronians (Scottish Rifles)*: the words, *"No special preference"* were stamped across my application form! This regiment had its roots in the Covenanters' movement.

Its origin can be traced back to *Richard Cameron.* Shortly after the Covenanters' disastrous defeat at Bothwell Bridge, Richard Cameron returned to Scotland. He and his followers openly opposed the king's forces, who were actively hunting down the Covenanters. Like William Wallace, Scotland's great military hero, he was killed: his head and hands were cut off and taken as a trophy to Edinburgh. He was only 32 years of age. His followers later, formed the nucleus of a new regiment, the *Cameronians (Scottish Rifles)*.

Prior to my period of National Service, I had become a Christian and, along with other new recruits, I was sent for training to the regiment's training barracks in Lanark: while there, I became aware of two traditions, rooted in the regiment's Covenanter history.

The first was the central place which the Bible had as the Covenanters' guide in life – each Company had a Bible placed in the senior officer's room – the regiment clearly pre-dated the *Gideons'* Bible placements.

The second tradition was more dramatic. On a chosen Sunday, new recruits were required to attend an unusual regimental church service in the local Parish Church. The service, which I attended, had a larger congregation than usual, as all soldiers were expected to attend.

Sentries, with rifles, were posted outside. Each one had to enter - no doubt after a thorough search for enemy soldiers! - And declare: "*No enemy in sight*", before the service could begin.

This service commemorated the practice, of the persecuted Covenanters, of holding their own unlawful services - although these were more often held in solitary places than in churches. The more militant element, carried arms to defend themselves from attack should the government's forces arrive to disband them.

By this time, I was a 20th Century "Covenanter", in my fundamental beliefs – less of the extreme element perhaps and more conciliatory by persuasion. In true Covenanter spirit, I prayed by my bedside in the barrack room – but not all my fellow soldiers appeared to appreciate my covenanter zeal!

**

A short history of events, including the Reformation, leading to the emergence of the Covenanters.

The history of the Covenanters has as its backcloth, the re-discovery of the true biblical faith during the Reformation. Prior to this, in the *Dark Ages*, the church's head in Rome, the pope, was the ultimate authority in religious matters: saints and relics were worshipped and forgiveness of sins was based on payments in money or in kind. All services were conducted in Latin, and as the common people, and many of the clergy, did not understand Latin, they were "kept in the dark," as far as the teaching of the Bible was concerned.

But, great and far reaching changes were about to take place. For the first time, large sailing ships opened up new continents to international travel and trade and this was paralleled by equally significant changes in the *religious* world.

Martin Luther became deeply concerned about the practices of the Catholic Church, of which he was a member and chairman of Biblical Theology at the University of Wittenberg. In **1517**, he published his objections in the form of his *Ninety-Five Theses*, attaching them to the door of the Castle Church. In this way, he openly challenged some of the Church's practices, showing them to be contrary to the teaching of the New Testament. From Romans Chapter 1 and Ephesians Chapter 2, he demonstrated, that forgiveness of sins, was by faith alone, in Christ alone, based on Jesus death on the cross and resurrection and was a free gift from God to all who believe.

Luther lit a torch for the Truth in the medieval darkness, of Germany, which was later carried by **John Calvin** to Switzerland and **John Knox** to Scotland.

The Reformation message did not go unopposed and in Scotland, Mary Queen of Scots persecuted those who followed the Protestant faith. Two godly preachers, Patrick Hamilton, in 1528 and George Wishart in 1546 were burned at the stake for their beliefs. Knox and other reformers persuaded the Scottish Parliament to establish, in 1540, a reformed church – the Church of Scotland, based on the doctrine of *Justification by faith.*

But, other forces were also at work, prior to Luther's declaration of faith: these would prepare the way for the wider, *written* transmission of the re-discovered faith.

In the **1380's** – more than a century before Luther's declaration - **John Wycliffe**, an Oxford professor and theologian, produced a number of *hand-written* portions of the Bible in the English language .Wycliffe has rightly been described as the *"Morning Star* of the Reformation" - meaning, *heralding its coming.* His initiative was not welcomed by the existing authorities and one of his followers, John Huss, was burned at the stake in 1415.

Then, in 1450, **Johannes Gutenberg**, of Germany, *invented the printing press* and twenty six years later, **William Caxton** produced the first *printed* book in Britain.

William Tyndale was the first person to print the New Testament in English , *from the original Greek language,* in which it was written. He arranging for copies to be smuggled into Britain. Henry VIII ordered these to be destroyed. Tyndale was later betrayed and burned at the stake in 1536. His accurate translations were a key source document in the wording of the Authorised Version, of 1611.

King **Henry VIII** brought about a momentous step-change for the reformation, when he severed the Church of England's link with the Pope – not for reason of his faith, but because the Pope would not grant him a divorce from his first wife, Catherine of Aragon!

In 1532, exercising what he, and some other monarchs in

the years which followed his reign, believed to be *The Divine right of kings,* he appointed *himself as Head of the Church of England*, with the final say in matters spiritual! Some years later, Henry VIII, having sided with the reformers now encouraged the printing of Cranmer's Bible - the *Coverdale Great Bible.*

During the years which followed, Catholics and Protestants suffered persecution, depending on who ruled at the time.

In 1603, **King James I, of England** (VI of Scotland), son of Mary Queen of Scots, became king on the death of Queen Elizabeth I.

In his capacity as Head of the Church of England and as King, James I, in **1611**, authorised, the most popular and prized version of the Bible, the *King James Authorised Version (AV).*It is the product of the combined efforts of fifty scholars and is an excellent and reliable translation from the original languages. The authorisation, or *Dedication* as it is called, is located at the front of most *AV's.* The *Dedication* also contains a fawning acknowledgement of King James's "powers and attributes."

It was the exercise and abuse of this *Supreme authority in religious matters* by subsequent monarchs, which would give rise to the Covenanters' movement in Scotland and to years of suffering for many dissidents. The *Dedication* itself contained what would become the root of the Scottish Kirk and Covenanters' problems.

While seeking to be loyal to the reigning monarch, the Scottish Kirk recognised Christ alone as its supreme Head and its organisational structure was more democratic. The *Dedication,* authorised by James I, was written, however, from the Church of England's point of view and not that of the reformed Scottish Kirk.

In the *AV*, the word *elder* is translated *bishop* to conform to the organisational structure of the Church of England at that time. The king was the Head of the Church and authority was exercised by the Bishops. This was fine, as far as the Scottish Kirk was concerned – provided this structure was not imposed on them along with the Liturgies and Common Prayer Books adopted by the English Church. But, problems arose when these were imposed! This led to the Covenanters' resistance movement.

**

The Covenanters and their struggles

Unfortunately, **Charles I,** - who succeeded, his father, James I, after his death in 1625 -and the English Church's hierarchy, attempted to impose the Episcopal structure and its Liturgies on the Scottish Kirk. This led, in 1637, to the legendary incident recorded in St Giles, Edinburgh, when Jenny Geddes flung her three-legged stool at the dean shouting, "Dost thou say mass in my lug?"

A year later, as a protest, ministers of the Kirk, nobles and commoners drew up a *"National Covenant"* and signed it in Edinburgh. It was sent throughout Scotland to be signed by a large number of sympathisers, who by signing, pledged their allegiance to the king, and to *adhere to and defend the true religion*. The signatories became known as *"Covenanters."*

A second covenant was signed in 1643, reflecting their growing concern. It was called, *"The Solemn League and Covenant."* This was effectively an agreement between the Presbyterians in Scotland and Puritans in England to unite in defending the civil and religious liberties of the two countries. It made no mention of allegiance to the king.

When **Charles II,** returned to England to reclaim his throne, in **1660,** following on the death of Oliver Cromwell, he aggressively set out to impose the Episcopal structure throughout Britain, passing an Act, in 1662, requiring all ministers to adhere to the English system.

Ministers of the Scottish Kirk, who refused to comply, were ejected from office and church and forced to leave their homes and parish and live elsewhere. Episcopal *"Curates"* were brought in to take their place and introduce the English form of service.

William Hamilton, the Glassford Kirk minister was forcibly ejected from his charge and replaced by Mr Findlay, an Episcopal curate, who acted in this capacity from 1662-1672.

Over 300 of the Scottish ministers, refused to comply with Parliament's orders and they, and their followers, held services in secret, in the open air, often in wind-swept, isolated places, in the countryside. These gatherings or *"Conventicles,"* were forbidden by law. The king ordered his troops to disband them and heavy financial penalties were enforced on sympathisers and all who refused to recant. Many were brutally treated and imprisoned, tortured and hanged or deported to the colonies.

It is against this background, that stories have been told about one of the most infamous perpetrators of these crimes, John Graham of Claverhouse ("Bloody Claverhouse"), leader of the king's dragoons and referred to by them, as "Bonnie Dundee." He is the notorious villain in Sir Walter Scott's book, *"Old Mortality,"* which I referred to earlier; and his cruel actions were frequently the subject of *"Recitations"* at Christian Brethren informal occasions, in Scotland.

Many Covenanters sought their religious freedom peacefully, while still being loyal to the monarchy, but others, like Richard Cameron, carried weapons to defend themselves and were more extreme in their methods in seeking to obtain their objectives.

The latter part of **Charles II's** reign and that of his successor, and brother, the Duke of York, who became **James II**, led to great violence and armed conflict between the king's forces and the Covenanters.

**

Covenanter battles and the Local Situation in Glassford and Chapelton

When the government, under Charles II, employed the military to disband the Conventicles, an incident took place in Galloway. This brought about the first armed conflict and several hundred armed covenanters marched towards Edinburgh. They were defeated by the government's forces at the **battle of Rullion Green** just outside Edinburgh, in the Pentland Hills, in **1666**.

Local records show that, that three Glassford men – Robert Semple (Craigthorn), William Semple (Whitecraig) and William Marshall (Four Pennyland) – were involved in the battle of Rullion Green, and killed, or mortally wounded, in defence of their faith. John Hart (Westquarter, an earlier name for Glassford) was apprehended later, in his home, and executed. Some of these names and places will still be familiar to local people even today.

These were but "the beginning of sorrows" for the reformers.

A second battle took place, at *Drumclog,* thirteen years after the battle of Rullion Green. It was significant in that it led, three weeks later, to the largest armed conflict in the Covenanters' history and to their final, decisive, military defeat. This, in turn, led to the *"Killing Time"* of the 1680's and barbaric persecution of the Covenanters.

The **battle of Drumclog**, took place on *1 June* **1679.**

John Graham of Claverhouse received news that a Conventicle was being held, near Loudon Hill, and when he arrived there with his troops, they were surprised to find armed Covenanters, guarding the approach to the service. There were around 250 armed men, 50 of them on horses. William Cleland, who was later to play a leading role in the formation of the *Cameronians (Scottish Rifles)* regiment, was in charge of the foot soldiers.

Claverhouse commanded his troops to open fire, but the soldiers anticipating this, quickly fell to the ground, and largely escaped unharmed.

Claverhouse, was unaware that the ground before him was very boggy. He ordered his horsemen to attack and the horses quickly became mired in the bog. The Covenanters, seizing their opportunity, advanced on Claverhouse's dragoons, with the cry of: "*Over the bog and at them men.*" - A cry attributed to a Mr Nisbet – of whom more later, under my heading, "*The Covenanters and the Quakers.*" They succeeded in killing a number of Claverhouse's men, and his dragoons fled.

News of the victory spread through south Scotland and beyond and many Covenanters, hearing of the victory, armed themselves for battle, and headed for Bothwell Bridge. By the first week in June, thousands of armed men gathered, between Bothwell and Hamilton, on the west of the river Clyde.

The Battle of **Bothwell Bridge.** *Sunday 22 June* **1679.**

The tragic battle – from the point of view of the Covenanters – is well documented. Shortly before the battle began, the king had sent the Duke of Monmouth, a moderate, to take command of the government's forces and he advanced with his army from the opposite side of Bothwell Bridge. John Graham of Claverhouse was an officer in his army.

Some of the more moderate Covenanters sent a deputation to Monmouth seeking peace terms and greater freedom of worship but this was offered on the grounds that the Covenanters laid down their weapons, which they refused to do.

Charles II had passed an Act of Indulgence in 1669 allowing ministers to return to office in the Kirk, without having to resort to full Episcopal authority; the Act was promoted, not so much out of tolerance but, to obtain his political objectives. The acceptance or rejection by ministers of the Indulgence was to prove a major bone of contention among the ranks of the Covenanters, greatly reducing their superiority in numbers over the government's forces. Many became disheartened and returned home. Theological debating and bad leadership were no doubt two of the major factors leading to the final, defeat of the Covenanters at the Battle of Bothwell Bridge.

It is estimated that on the day of battle, the king's well trained army, numbering around 5000, now exceeded that of the poorly, led, trained and equipped Covenanters, whose forces were, by now, substantially reduced to around 4000 and they possessed only one small canon and muskets to defend the passageway across the bridge.

At the centre of the narrow bridge was a portal with gates and the Covenanter army had built a barricade there, where 300 of the bravest of the Covenanters sought to defend this critical point on the bridge but, being desperately short of ammunition they were quickly swept aside by the oncoming forces. By mid-morning, the battle was over and the Covenanters defeated. Around 400 men were killed in the immediate battle and more than 1200 were taken prisoner.

Times of "greater tribulation" were to follow.

The Covenanters, who were alive and captured, were taken to Edinburgh and imprisoned. For more than four months, they were poorly fed and those who were confined outside were exposed to inclement weather. While many died as prisoners, some were set free when they swore never again to take up arms or disobey the king's commands: only a small number remained, refusing to give up their faith or accept the terms of release. They were sentenced to be sold as slaves in the West Indies.

Placed in the hold of a ship, which set sail in December, most were drowned when the ship was broken by a storm off the Orkney coast and only a handful escaped.

There is no record that I am aware of, of the names of local men, who no doubt were immediately associated with the battle but, two *Glassford* men, James Scoular and Gavin Semple are recorded as having gone towards Hamilton "to listen to a sermon", on the day on which the battle took place, and on the way there, they were killed.

The "Killing Time", of the 1680's.

The *killing Time* was the term given to the terrible suffering endured by Covenanters at the hands of the Government forces, following on the defeat at Bothwell Bridge.

James, Duke of York, Charles II's brother, was appointed High Commissioner to the Scottish Parliament in 1680. He began to introduce measures against all who held to the Protestant faith. The persecution intensified, when he became **King James II** (VII of Scotland) in 1685, on the death of Charles II.

James introduced fresh legislation, which was passed by the Scottish Parliament, declaring the Episcopal system as the required form of Church government, making it treasonable to defend the Covenants and the death penalty was decreed for those who held field meetings. The resulting persecution included payment of fines, confiscation of property, beatings, imprisonment, executions and deportations.

Again, turning to the *local situation*, a few *examples* of the Glassford and Chapelton men and women who suffered for their faith and refusal to conform to the dictates of King and Parliament, during this period, are given below:

In Glassford, in 1683, Michael Marshall and John Kay were imprisoned then banished to New Jersey, America.

In 1684, John Semple (Craigthorn) was taken by soldiers to Hamilton Tolbooth, - perhaps because of his suspected role in the Battle of Bothwell Bridge - where he had his fingers driven into the *"thummeking"* and his legs into bolts, enduring both at the same time, for 5 hours, in order to increase his torments. Later, in Edinburgh, he was sentenced to death and executed. Like the martyr, Stephen, in the New Testament, being well-versed in the Scriptures and of strong faith, he was able to confound his questioners and bear his sufferings patiently.

One of his sisters visited him, while he was imprisoned in Edinburgh, "*to put on his dead clothes.*" She herself was imprisoned for caring for her brother and her mother, Janet Scott, came to see her in prison and was herself imprisoned. Both women were later sentenced to be deported to America but the sentence was not carried out and they spent between two and three years in prison. So this loyal family all suffered for their faith.

In Chapelton , in 1685 a number of Chapelton men were apprehended at the instigation of Lord Glasford, for allegedly having entertained armed rebels and having borne arms themselves against the government. Their legal expenses, to defend themselves, were onerous: but despite summoning a number of witnesses against them, the case was not proven and they were set free, having suffered imprisonment in Edinburgh for two weeks. These men were listed as: "Alexander Hamilton and John Struthers (Shawtonhill); John Semple (Shawton); John Fleeming, John Walker, James Scott, John Paterson, John Marshall (senior and junior), James Lowrie (all from Chapelton); and John and William Semple and Gavin Paterson from Nethershields.

**

During the 1680's, the Test Act had also been passed by James, Duke of York and the Scottish Parliament and those, who occupied a position in the Church or State were required to sign their allegiance to the King and the Episcopal religion. Those who refused to do so were dismissed from their posts. Also, during the period 1682 - 1684, a second curate had been appointed to the Glassford Kirk, a Mr Davidson.

Again, there is a local record of Glassford and Chapelton men and women who suffered in refusing to comply.

In Glassford, John Alston of Glassford Mill spent 6 months in Glasgow Tolbooth for refusing the test:

In Chapelton, John Fleeming, Elder, was imprisoned in various places for a total of thirty-four weeks for refusing the test and was sentenced to be banished to America but the sentence was not carried out.

Thomas Fleeming in Chapelton went to hear field preachers and had an inventory of his goods taken with a view to seizing them.

Also Alexander Hamilton in Shawtonhill was imprisoned in Glasgow tollbooth for a month, because it was alleged that he had attended a Conventicle.

John Alston, Elder, *in Glassford* was fined three dollars for failing to have his child baptised (christened) by the curate.

Some men were punished because their *wives* did not attend to hear the Glassford curate: these included, John Marshall (Heads), who was imprisoned 14 days in Hamilton tollbooth and Gavin Paterson in Nethershields, who was fined three dollars.

Ann Semple Watt (in Croutherland) was herself imprisoned 14 days in Hamilton for not attending to listen to the Curate.

The above named, are some of the recorded, local examples of those who suffered for their faith and for refusing to conform to the dictates of king and parliament. There are many stories of Covenanter persecutions throughout south of Scotland and many graveyards today mark places where Covenanters were buried.

The *Killing Time* was brought to an end, when King James II's daughter Mary and her Dutch husband, **William of Orange,** defeated James's army at the **Battle of Boyne,** in **1689.**

Scotland's special Christian heritage came down to us at great cost, stained by the blood and sacrifice of faithful people. What value do we place on such examples of sacrifice today?

The New Testament, in Hebrews Chapter 11, provides a list of men and women, "heroes of the faith", down through history, **before the birth of Jesus.** It was recorded to challenge the followers of Jesus to live out their faith. The supreme example of suffering for others completes the list in Chapter 11 and reads: *"looking unto Jesus the author and finisher of our faith, who for the joy that was set before Him, endured the cross, despising the shame and is set down at the right hand of the throne of God."(Chapter 12, verse 2).*

** **

The Martyr's Monument, in the old section of the Glassford Graveyard.

I have already mentioned the words, which I read, on the Martyr's Monument: *"If a hard fate demands or claims a tear, stay gentle passenger and shed it here."* I can now provide the answer to my youthful curiosity regarding who the martyr was; where and when he died and who arranged the monument's erection.

The Martyr's Monument marks the burial place of William Gordon of Earlston. Earlston Castle is situated close to Earlston loch just north of Dalry in Galloway.

The Gordon family were closely associated with the Reformation and the Covenanters. William Gordon's father was one of the leaders who opposed the imposition, of an Episcopal minister in the parish of Dalry in 1635.

When his father died, William continued his father's opposition to Episcopacy, and was banished from Britain. He returned to take part in the battle of Bothwell Bridge, when he was 65 years of age. On the way to the battlefield, with his son Alexander, William was killed by the government's forces, on the old Hamilton Road. Alexander escaped and fled to a friend's house with the soldiers in hot pursuit.

Legend has it, that in the house, he was disguised and dressed as a woman, and when his pursuers arrived, they found only a woman sitting rocking a baby's cradle. Outside, the householder was removing the tell-tale, Covenanters' insignia from Alexander's horse. The incident has shades of "Bonnie Prince Charlie" about it!

Alexander was forced to flee to the Continent, but was later captured and tortured, when he returned. His family were evicted from their home.

The night his father William was shot, friends took William's body and buried it in the Glassford graveyard. A stone was erected, but no Covenanter's name was permitted by law to be added to the stone.

The following inscription was added to the Monument, almost 100 years later by his great-grandson. *"To the memory of the very worthy Pillar of the Church, Mr William Gordon of Earlston, in Galloway, shot by a party of dragoons on his way to Bothwell Bridge, 22 June 1679, aged 65. Inscribed by his great-grandson, Sir John Gordon, Bart., 11 June 1772.*

**

Covenanters and the Quakers

How I would like to have concluded my story of the Covenanters, with a picture of tolerance towards other dissident groups, such as the *Quakers.* But it was not so – at least as far as some of the more militant elements of the Covenanters were concerned.

The Covenanters were prepared to defend the Truth with their lives, but despite the sufferings which they endured, many were intolerant towards Quakers.

The following are two *local examples* of hostility towards the early Quakers, who were regarded as heretics and suffered greatly for their beliefs.

On one occasion, James Naismith, minister of Glasford Parish Church, summoned **John Hart,** *a leading Quaker from the Heads*, and another Quaker, to appear before the Presbytery of Hamilton for "holding and spreading the heretical doctrines of the Quakers." Rev. Bill Stewart describes him as one of, *"The shakers of the Quakers!"* He further commented that the action of this minister led to persecution of the Quakers by Glassford villagers, who disrupted Quaker meetings, burned down their buildings and attacked them. And this was not the first harassment suffered by these local Quakers.

I mentioned earlier, that I would come back to **John Nisbet**, a prominent leader in the Covenanters' victory at the battle of Drumclog and later at the Battle of Bothwell Bridge. I do so now.

He and his followers attacked the home of Robert Hamilton, a Quaker at Shawton, *Chapelton*, and killed him. They then vandalised and desecrated the Quakers' new burial ground in Chapelton.

* *

QUAKERS

Parochial records

As a teenager, I had heard rumours of Quaker activities, at one time in the past, in or near Glassford, but could not find any evidence to back these up: nor was I aware, at that time, of the existence of a Quaker burial ground in Chapelton. As I was to discover, in my researches for this part of my book, the "sons of the manse" seemed, until recently, to be the sole repositories of such local knowledge, and for the layman, there was no easy access to their "Parochial records" – no criticism intended - it was the way it was. Indeed, without the Kirk ministers and the Kirk Sessions' efforts to record local events, there would have been no local story to tell.

But the Quakers were in the area, in significant numbers, at the outset of the Quaker movement, located in the **Heads (Glassford)**, around **1653**. Twenty-one members were enrolled, meeting in the home of **John Hart**, who I mentioned earlier, was being targeted by James Naismith, minister at Glassford at that time, for "*holding and spreading the heretical doctrines of the Quakers.*" One of the founder leaders of the Quakers, George Fox appears to have visited the group on three occasions to encourage them.

Just as in the Bible story of the feeding of the five thousand, *besides women and children,* there may have been more than 21 attendees.

The Rev Gavin Lang, in July 1835, mentions in his comments on the *"Parochial Economy,"* that the Glassford Parish contained three villages, Westquarter (which later changed its name to Glassford); Chapelton and Heads and that, their respective populations were 501, 558 and 68. I was surprised by these figures because, when I was living in the locality, Glassford had the largest population; Chapelton had significantly fewer people than Glassford and the Heads consisted of two small farms and a few cottages. We considered it to be part of Glassford. What these figures show is that 21 Quakers meeting in an area with a small population must have had a significant impact.

**

Beginning of the Quaker movement and early beliefs

The Covenanters was a *short term protest movement,* in *Scotland,* arising largely as a consequence of outside interference in their structure and mode of worship.

The Quakers, on the other hand, was a *permanent* movement, beginning in *England,* around the same time as the Covenanters and passing through the same difficult period of civil and political strife.

The key founder of the Quakers, George Fox, dissatisfied with the shallowness of the State Church; the corruption he saw around him and his inability to put right what was wrong in his own life, spent long periods, alone, with his Bible, seeking an answer to his problems. In his spiritual quest, (recorded in detail in his *George Fox Journal, 1694)* he came to believe that Jesus teaching could only be made effective, through direct, personal communion with God and by God's continuing revelation to him. He described this as the *inner light* in every man.

He and his followers, believed that, while the Bible is important, and accepted as part of God's revelation, in the ultimate, as the inner light, the Lord Jesus Christ still reveals Himself to the individual today. The early Quakers believed that Christ would not lead them in ways which would contradict the Bible.

But the dichotomy between direct revelation through the

inner light or *inward Christ* and the Bible as the only source of divine inspiration and authority, would lead to later polarisation within the Quaker movement. The Quakers were regarded as heretics, by the other newly emerging, reformed groups and by the king and the State Church.

James, in his New Testament epistle, states that Abraham was called the *Friend* of God. Jesus, while on earth used the word *friends* to describe His disciples. "*Friends*" is the word Quakers use to describe themselves.

James also states, that, "*Abraham was made righteous before God because he believed*" (i.e. by Faith). This is the only way, according to God's Word, by which we can be made right with God. The Covenanters were clear on this: but the Quakers in practice were more concerned with religious experience than with creedal statements. Their emphasis was on the living out of Jesus teaching in everyday life.

James also teaches that, "*faith without works is dead*", and that Abraham showed the reality of his faith by his actions. The Quaker movement, in the two centuries which followed, made a prodigious contribution to the welfare of humankind.

John Bunyan, author of *Pilgrim's Progress* entered into lengthy, often heated, written, debates with some of the Quakers' early leaders regarding their reliance on their inner light, rather than on God's Written Word, the Bible.

Bunyan too, lived, *in England,* through the same period of turmoil as the Covenanters and Quakers. He spent 12 years in jail, from 1660, when Charles II was made king after the death of Cromwell. He refused to give up preaching or to conform, (a freedom he had enjoyed under the Puritan Commonwealth). Interestingly, he was set free by Charles II, when the Quakers included Bunyan's name in their list of jailed non-conformists in 1672! He died in 1688, a few months before the "glorious revolution" under King William of Orange in 1689.

Jesus had taught, in the Sermon on the Mount, the importance of speaking the truth *at all times*. And based on His words, the *Friends* refused to *swear an oath* in court proceedings, believing that to do so implied different standards of truthfulness from the norm: they also refused to swear an oath of loyalty to Cromwell or the King.

Believing that everyone was *equal* in the sight of God, they refused to "take off their hats," as a symbol of respect to those in higher office: instead, they addressed everyone, irrespective of rank or office, by their common name. As the movement grew, it majored on *peace* and *brotherly love*. *Friends* refused to take up arms to defend themselves or go to war.

The reasons for these actions were largely misunderstood by the authorities, and many Quakers suffered beatings, imprisonments, torture and some were hanged, while others were banished to the new colonies in America. It is characteristic of the Quakers that despite their own sufferings in prisons, they were among the first to seek improved prison conditions for others.

The Quakers openly opposed the need for consecrated buildings, ordained officials, religious symbols and sacraments in whatever religious form. Like other dissenters, they refused to attend worship services in the State Church, even when required to do, by those in authority. Their public protests led to frequent clashes with the authorities.

The Quaker numbers grew rapidly and by 1660, they numbered around 20,000. George Fox regularly attracted crowds, often in large numbers – when he was not in prison for illegally preaching in the open air.

**

The Quakers' legacy

The early Quakers expressed their beliefs and practices in the form of *Testimonies* and *Annual Meetings* were held by them in London.

In 1694, Penn published, "*The rise and Progress of the People called Quakers*" as a preface to George Fox's *Journal,* setting out their Testimonies. These included, their loving care for one another (*brotherly love*); loving their enemies - they do not fight and are willing to suffer instead,(*peace*); telling the truth without taking oaths or swearing (*integrity*); not showing respect to authorities more than to any other persons (*equality*); abstaining from drinking alcohol (*sobriety)*and practicing silence during worship – they waited on God.

Luke Johnson, (the then chairman of Channel 4, TV) in an article in the Financial Times, dated 11th July 2007, summed up the extraordinary, beneficial, impact which the Quakers had on industry and commerce in Britain in the past two hundred years: "*The foundation of much of our industrial revolution was laid by just .2 per cent of the population*" - *the Quakers.*" He went on to list Cadbury, Rowantree and Fry, our great chocolate makers, as having been founded by the Quakers – was this partly because they saw hot chocolate as an alternative to alcoholic beverage?

His list of Quaker founded enterprises included, Lloyds and Barclays (two of our major clearing banks), GlaxoSmithKline, our largest pharmaceutical company, Bryant and May (matchmakers), Ransomes (lawn mowers) Reckitt & Colman (mustard makers). An impressive list.

He also named the famous Abraham Darby who, "*founded an iron dynasty by creating the first coke consuming blast furnace in 1709 and Edward Pease, who opened the first modern railway in 1825,"* and others who contributed to the Industrial Revolution in Britain.

It is beyond the scope of this book to enter in detail into the major role played by the Quakers, who were among the first to recognise the evils of slavery in Britain and America and take action to abolish the trade. But, in 1783, the London Yearly Meeting of Quakers petitioned Parliament and reaching out beyond their own sect the Quakers established a non-*sectarian Society for Effecting the Abolition of the Slave Trade.* Their actions coincided with initiatives from the Evangelical Anglicans. John Wesley, (evangelist) and William Cowper (Christian poet) were also supportive.

After slavery was abolished in the Northern States of America, it persisted in the South. Again the Quakers were prominent in operating the network of safe houses and escape routes for Southern slaves, known as the *Underground Railroad.* In 1947, the Quakers were awarded the Nobel Peace Prize for their world-wide efforts in promoting *peace.*

I have outlined some of the areas in which the Quakers, over the centuries, have sought to put into practise the teaching of Jesus, in His *Sermon on the Mount*: in doing so they have gained enormous respect from those who have observed their activities. In this they have sought to *walk the talk*, even if sadly many appear to have lost touch with the importance of the doctrines for which the Covenanters were prepared to sacrifice their lives.

**

Quakers today and a local story
Today I am not aware of any Quaker activities in Glassford or Chapelton. They do however at the time of my writing, appear to meet in the Citadel in Ayr, and have various meeting places throughout Scotland.

Just outside the Booths car park in Keswick, in the Lake District, where we holiday most years, there is a Quakers' meeting place and on a recent visit to Durham, my son Alistair noticed the evidence of current Quaker activities. It was in Yorkshire and the Lake District that the Quaker movement began.

The movement today, is worldwide, with well over $\frac{1}{4}$ million members. In America there are a number of different groupings including a strong evangelical group, whose beliefs appear to embrace the major doctrines of other evangelical churches: there are other groups which are extremely liberal which have no creed or formulation of faith, embracing all who profess a religion and those who don't but, who seek the inner light.

** **

I come back now to my first evidence of Quaker activities in the area where I grew up. I visited for the first time, with David Kinnaird, the Quakers' graveyard in Chapelton, on the Shawton Road on the outskirts of the village.

I commented earlier about the local opposition to the Quakers on the part of the Scottish Kirk and the militant Covenanters. Because they were viewed as heretics by the Scottish Kirk, they had to purchase this piece of land as a burial ground. A sign was later erected there bearing the words, "*Society of Friends, Quakers burying ground 1675.*" Under the original purchase deed, the local farmer has to maintain the boundary walls.

As David and I entered the burial ground, we were surprised when a car drew up and a woman in her mid-nineties, *Jenny Aird,* appeared and asked why we were visiting the burial ground. She lives in East Kilbride and 'keeps her eye on the place.'

Only one modest stone can now be seen and it is sinking into the ground, where other stones now lie buried. It marks the burial place of the last Quaker to be buried there. Even in the matter of burials, the Quakers treated all their members as equal and all stones are of a modest nature being of the same size and generally, facing in the same direction.

This particular burial ground is no longer in use. The stone marks the burial place of *Robert **Barclay** Murdoch who died in 1932*- two years before I was born. Jenny informed us that he had something to do with the founding of Barclays Bank. I leave that story to interested readers to follow up.

I searched the internet for information on the founding of Barclays Bank. The Bank went through a number of stages in its early formation – and sure enough, the Quakers were involved in founding it.

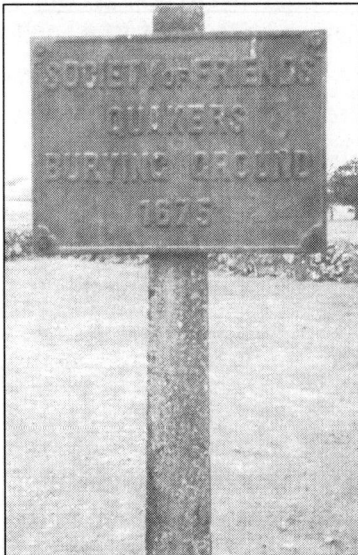

Quakers graveyard showing
date of origin.

Quakers graveyard.

MAP 1

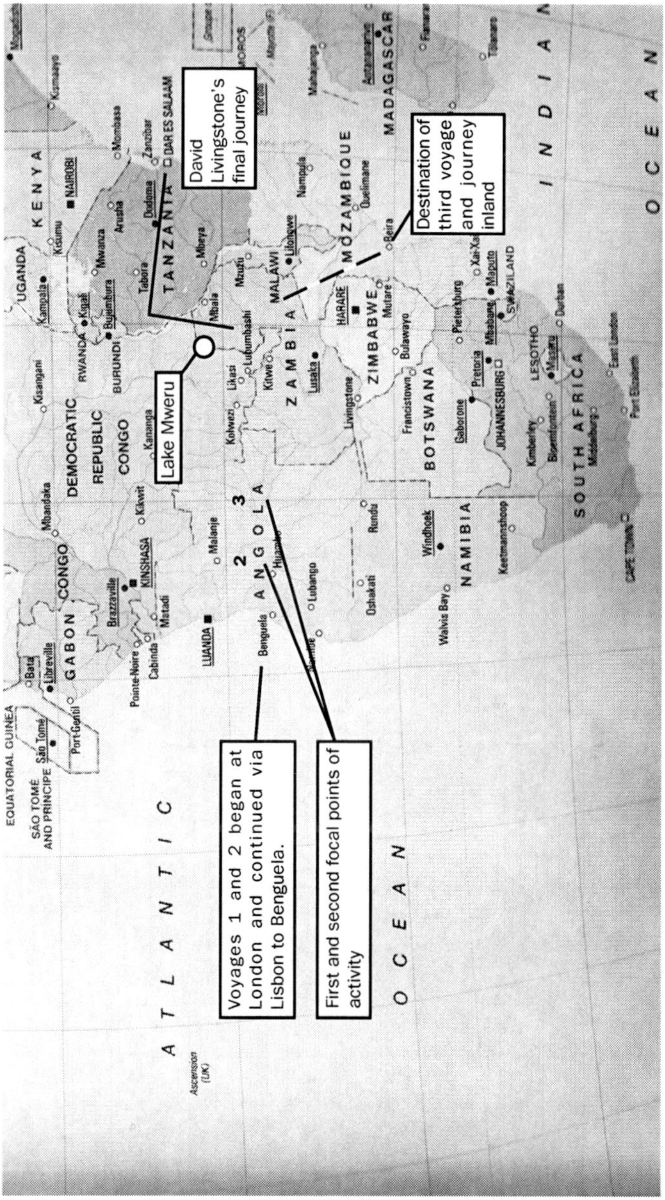
David Livingstone's final journey
Lake Mweru
Destination of third voyage and journey inland
Voyages 1 and 2 began at London and continued via Lisbon to Benguela.
First and second focal points of activity
1
2
3
A T L A N T I C
O C E A N
I N D I A N
O C E A N
ANGOLA
ZAMBIA
TANZANIA
MOZAMBIQUE
MADAGASCAR
KENYA
UGANDA
RWANDA
BURUNDI
DEMOCRATIC REPUBLIC CONGO
CONGO
GABON
MALAWI
ZIMBABWE
BOTSWANA
NAMIBIA
SOUTH AFRICA
LESOTHO
SWAZILAND
EQUATORIAL GUINEA
SÃO TOMÉ AND PRINCIPE
LUANDA
Benguela
KINSHASA
HARARE
DAR ES SALAAM
NAIROBI
Lusaka
Beira

Modern Map of Central Africa

MAP 2

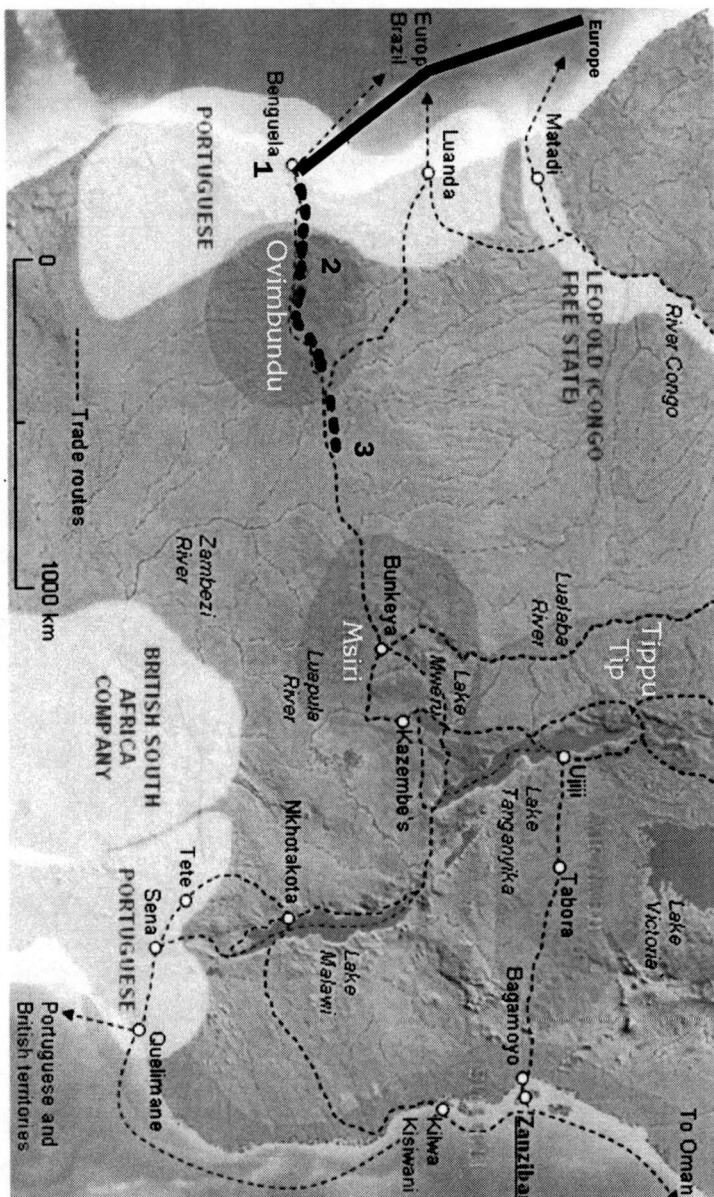

Central Africa, 1880's – Msiri's Kingdom

------ Trade routes

0   1000 km

PORTUGUESE

Benguela 1

Ovimbundu

2

3

Europe/Brazil

Europe

Luanda

Matadi

Europe

LEOPOLD (CONGO FREE STATE)

River Congo

Zambezi River

BRITISH SOUTH AFRICA COMPANY

Bunkeya

Msiri

Luapula River

Lualaba River

Lake Mweru

Kazembe's

Tippu Tip

Lake Tanganyika

Ujiji

Tabora

Lake Victoria

Nkhotakota

Lake Malawi

Tete

Sena

PORTUGUESE

Quelimane

Portuguese and British territories

Kilwa

Kiswani

Zanzibar

Bagamoyo

To Oman

PART TWO
From Chapelton to Central Africa:
the Jeanie Gilchrist story.

THE 1859 REVIVAL

This Revival first began in the United States of America, in 1858 and spread to Ireland, and Great Britain.

Prior to the outbreak of the Revival, America although prosperous was in spiritual decline. The period of financial prosperity was arrested by a severe financial crisis, forcing many businesses to close down, while unemployment soared: much like the situation today during the current "Credit Crunch".

Jeremiah Lanphier, a businessman, advertised in New York for other businessmen to join him every Wednesday to pray. On the first evening, only six attended: but God was at work and within six months, 10,000 people were meeting daily for prayer, in New York.

Revival broke out in 1858 and within two years leading newspapers estimated that, around one million people had become Christians. D.L. Moody, the world famous evangelist was a young man at the time and was greatly influenced by the Revival. He started a Sunday school for children, which soon numbered 1500 a week.

The *Ulster Revival* began in 1859. Southern Ireland too was greatly blessed: C.H. Spurgeon preached to crowded meetings in Dublin and many became followers of Christ.

Revival spread to *Scotland and other parts of Britain* in 1859.

A number of well-known British hymn-writers lived during the time of the Revival, including *Charlotte Elliott* who wrote the hymn, "*Just as I am, without one plea,*" in 1834. This hymn has been greatly used of God in Christian outreach and in Gospel Campaigns throughout the world, even to the present day. *Frances Ridley Havergale,* as a young girl, wrote the words of her first and perhaps greatest hymn in 1859, the year of the Revival: "*Take my life and let it be,* consecrated *Lord to Thee.*"

Even before the Revival impacted Scotland, the country was already greatly influenced by such godly men of prayer as *Horatius and Andrew Bonar and Murray McCheyne.*

Horatius was a prolific hymn-writer. His hymns are numbered in the hundreds and many were written for children.

Robert Murray McCheyne was a minister in Dundee, and his godly living and preaching had a great impact on his large congregation, with many turning to God. He had to retire because of ill-health and his successor, W.C Bruce benefited greatly from McCheyne's influence, when a Revival broke out in Dundee in 1839.

Many came to trust in the Lord throughout Central and Southern Scotland as a result of the preaching of *M'Cheyne* and *Andrew Bonar.*

The Revival of 1859 created a missionary zeal, throughout Scotland and many were moved to bring the message of the gospel to those who had never heard it before.

Among those who went forth was *Hudson Taylor,* founder of the China Inland Mission, – and what a wonderful story his is of believing and answered prayer. He prayed to God that 100 missionaries would volunteer to go to China and his prayer were specifically answered. The book, "*The spiritual secrets of Hudson Taylor"* had a profound impact on my young life, causing me to seek a closer walk with God.

This Revival affected the lives of men, women and children throughout many areas of Scotland. It produced a profound, lasting and far reaching effect on the lives of two members of the Gilchrist family, in Chapelton, Lanarkshire – *James Gilchrist* and his daughter Jeanie. *Jeanie Gilchrist of Chapelton* was one of those who responded to the missionary call.

The Revival also marked the beginning of the Christian Brethren Assemblies in Lanarkshire.

**

Primary source of the story of James Gilchrist and the early life of his daughter Jeanie.

The main source of the story of James Gilchrist and of the early life of his daughter Jeanie is an undated, red, hard-backed book, published by John Ritchie (of "John Ritchie, Publisher of Christian Literature, Kilmarnock", Ayrshire) around 1910, and out of print, for many years.

It has the initials *J.R.* in a "*Prefatory Note"* and has the title, "JEANIE GILCHRIST", on its front cover: the inside page adds the words, "PIONEER MISSIONARY TO THE WOMEN OF CENTRAL AFRICA."

I became aware of the book's existence, while a young member of the Christian Brethren, meeting in the *"Shiloh Hall",* in Glassford.

During regular visits to nearby Chapelton, where, once a month, we held gospel services in the public hall, I remember wishing to learn more about James Gilchrist, the local baker and publican, who had once conducted his business in the shop in the centre of the village, who had become a Christian during the 1859 Revival and whose daughter had become a missionary to Central Africa - the local missionary!

But, it was only when I started to research material for this part of the book that I was able to read their stories, for the first time, when the book was loaned to me by David and Martha for this purpose.

From this point onwards, I shall simply refer to it as *"JR's Book"*.

** **

THE CONVERSION OF JAMES GILCHRIST OF CHAPELTON

James Gilchrist was the village baker in Chapelton, but his premises in the centre of the village also became a public house, licensed to sell alcohol. It was the centre of attraction, not only for the village, but for many farm labourers and miners from the surrounding countryside, who "*came to dance and revel in Saturdays until a late hour.*"

James was deeply affected by the 1859 revival and after "*deep soul searching*", he accepted Jesus Christ as his Saviour and Lord. The transformation in his life was immediate and revolutionary. The day after his conversion, he entered his public house and "*stood condemned as he faced his whisky barrels.*" What a shock the villagers got when they saw him empty the contents of the barrels into the gutter and proceed to paint out the existing sign above the door of his premises with black paint. The sign had read, "*James Gilchrist, Publican*".

News of his actions quickly spread around the village and many thought "*the baker has gone mad!*"

It is my desire that all the villagers in Chapelton will become aware of this great event, which took place at the heart of their village.

James turned his premises into a "*gospel meeting and daily the message of the gospel was sounded forth in word and song.*" People came from far and near to see the transformed premises and witness the changed life of the village baker. The "*dancing hall*" became "*the gospel hall*" and for many years, the gospel was preached in Chapelton and through his preaching many came to accept Jesus Christ as their personal Saviour, including members of James's large family.

His preaching was not confined to Chapelton and he and three other men, including Alexander Taylor of Strathaven, frequently drove long distances throughout Lanarkshire in James's pony and cart, (a customary method of transport at the time) singing hymns and preaching as they went. On at least one occasion, they displayed a banner with the word, "*Eternity*" on one side and *"Prepare to meet thy God,"* on the other. Such a method of presentation was appropriate to the time and it had a powerful effect on their hearers: many becoming converts to the Christian faith.

Gilchrist family - far left, James Gilchrist, father of Jeanie Gilchrist
Picture courtesy of Frances Martin.

Who was the Alexander Taylor, the baker, in Strathaven, who accompanied James Gilchrist in his pony and cart, in his public witness for Christ?

In the early 1950's, when I was in my late teens, there was a Miss Taylor, who owned a baker's shop in Strathaven. It is highly likely that she was a descendant of Alexander Taylor.

She was active in Christian outreach, with the Strathaven *Mission Hall* and was well-known and loved by all who knew her. Her Saturday night tea-meetings gathered crowds of young people –the thought of her cream buns still make my taste-buds tingle!

**

The late Alex Strang, Larkhall, compiled: *"The Centenary of Hebron Hall Assembly, Larkhall – 1866-1966"*, (which my brother-in-law, Professor Roy McLarty, sent to me just as I was finalising my book). Alex was the Assembly's Secretary and I knew him.

Larkhall Assembly became one of the largest and most influential Brethren Assemblies in Lanarkshire, during this period and interestingly, he lists a *"Chapelton Assembly"* as one of the earliest to be formed in Lanarkshire - directly as a result of the 1859 Revival. It was formed in 1863 (no doubt arising from James Gilchrist's conversion): with 20 members in fellowship. It moved to East Kilbride in 1864. An Assembly/Church was also started in nearby Strathaven in 1863, with 20 members.

This was at the outset of the Brethren Movement in Scotland and the UK and marked the re-discovery of the Word of God with all the zeal and love, which first attracted me to this movement after my conversion, in Glassford, in 1950.

In Alex's book he makes reference to a well publicised event where *"over a thousand people assembled on the banks of the river Avon to witness the first baptism by immersion"*. This was the river I mentioned earlier in connection with Glassford (page 10). *"The first candidates were nicknamed the "dippers".*

He also refers to James Gilchrist, as a frequent visitor and preacher in Larkhall during this early period. Like many new converts in the movement who were discovering new truths from God's Word, for the first time , he came across the teaching of believer's baptism in the New Testament and never before having witnessed such an event but wishing to obey his Lord, *he went to the water and baptised himself*!! Quite a character!

**

JEANIE GILCHRIST -
PIONEER MISSIONARY TO CENTRAL AFRICA

Jeanie life story prior to her departure as a missionary
Jeanie was the first Scottish female Christian Brethren missionary to go to Central Africa and she was born into the large family of James Gilchrist, in Chapelton.

Sometime after her father, James's conversion, the family moved to Hamilton and established a bakery there. They lived in what is now 24, 26 and 28 Woodside Walk, Hamilton: it was known as the *"Gilchrist Building."*

Jeanie Gilchrist in the Gilchrist Bakery - Top far left.

Jeanie herself became a Christian in 1875, while living with her uncle in Larkhall, Lanarkshire. She was then a member of the Free Church of Scotland, but later, while reading the Scriptures, she learned the teaching of baptism by immersion and joined with the Christian Brethren in

"*Baillie's Causeway,*", Hamilton. The Gospel Hall there was built in 1872, so Jeanie must have been there, not longer after the Hall was built.

At the time when she decided to become a member of this church, she was engaged to a young minister in the Free Church: but he did not share her convictions regarding her move. By mutual consent, they decided to call off the engagement. Clearly, God had other plans for her life, as a missionary in Africa, but she did not know of this at the time.

During the period the family lived in Hamilton, Jeanie cared for them and actively engaged in house to house visitation bringing the gospel to all who would listen.

In 1885, she moved to Portsmouth, where for two years, she became involved in visiting hospitals, and ships in the harbour, tending the sick and needy.

Her personal work in Hamilton and Portsmouth was preparing her for her work among women in Central Africa.

**

Methodology adopted in researching Jeanie's story

I began this part of my project by reading the *JR Book*: but I soon discovered problems associated with the fact that it was published around a century ago, about Jeanie's activities, beginning in Africa, 120 years ago, in a largely unexplored and uncharted continent – the region simply being referred to as **Central Africa**!

Hardly any of the *place names* mentioned, have their equivalent today. Many villages consisted of only a few primitive mud or wooden huts, with straw roofs, enclosed by wooden stakes and a narrow entrance, which could be closed at night to provide safety from tribal invaders, slave traders or wild animals. Some were named after the local village chief or his wife and records of this time contained a variety of spellings, as there was no written language there and the writer recorded names as they sounded.

How, I wondered, could I possibly unravel this and make it meaningful, particularly to young people without the missionary background, which I had enjoyed?

There was also the added complication that, since JR wrote his book, *the map of Africa has changed geographically and politically*, beyond recognition, a number of times over and is still subject to change. Also, the *JR Book*, had omitted, certain *key dates and on* one occasion one of the important dates was incorrect. This was perhaps not so important then, as Jeanie would be known to his readers, but was important to me, if I was to make this part of her life story meaningful for today's readers.

Although I have always had an interest in missionary work, I had no specialised knowledge to help me write this part of the book. I wasn't even sure, to begin with, from reading the book, which *countries, in Central Africa, Jeanie had worked in.*

I sought help from a number of sources.

Regarding the *names of places* in the *JR Book,* I contacted *Interlink,* the Scottish Brethren missionary organisation, who contacted *Echoes of Service*, in England; and Hugh Reid of Motherwell, contacted his sister, Jean Kruse, retired missionary from Zambia. Together, they were able to throw sufficient light on some of the place names which, after further investigation, enabled me to resolve this particular problem. I also discovered there were various spelling of *places and people* (including tribal chiefs at that time) and I have spared the reader by rationalising these. Jeanie's name itself is variously spelt but JR's Book seems to have got it right!

Jane Cox's email from Echoes of Service to Ruth Blair in Interlink sums up the difficulties involved in identifying some of the original place names: *"After two hours of map reading, I think I now know most of the towns and villages of Angola, Zambia and DR of Congo!! I am now off to lie down!"*

Another unexpected helper was Frances Martin of Ayr, who happened to be tracing her family tree, on the Gilchrist side, at the same time as I was researching this part of the book. She had identified *Jeanie's date of birth* and other interesting facts about the Gilchrist connection: so now I was able to put Jeanie's story in a proper time-setting.

I am most grateful for the help given by the above.

I was also able to clarify and add to *JR's* excellent book, by cross referencing it to records of other male missionaries, who were better known than Jeanie and ,who played a leading role in missionary activities in Central Africa.

Then again, I was able to view Jeanie's journeys, from the added perspective of the 21st Century, having additional knowledge of other events which occurred during the time of Jeanie's visits, and since *JR's book* was written, about Central Africa, a century ago.

Records of better known, male missionaries, operating in Central Africa around the same period as Jeanie, are still available and one of my objectives was to add to these by producing an *up-dated* record of Jeanie's contribution. In doing so, I determined to produce a map(s) showing her journeys to Africa and where she worked when there.

In this respect, I was fortunate in finding a recently researched map, not in any way connected to Jeanie's story, showing, *inter alia*, trade routes, major tribes and *tribal chiefs* and identifying the growing *colonial powers*, across Central

Africa during the period of her pioneering work there – one of the tribal chiefs is mentioned in JR's book. This additional piece of history adds an interesting new element to Jeanie's missionary story and I have introduced an *Interlude* section to cover this.

I have also produced a *modern map of part of Africa*, tracing her journeys to and in Africa during her time as a missionary there.

**

Jeanie's call to the mission field and how it related to that of some other key Scottish missionaries to Central Africa - all, but one, were members of *the Christian Brethren.*

David Livingstone (Congregational Church), originated from Blantyre, near Hamilton and while he was not an associate working with Jeanie, as were the other Scottish missionaries mentioned in this section, his final explorations were carried out in the East part of Central Africa. He died there in 1873, in Tanzania.

During one of Livingstone's visits to the town of Hamilton, to give an account of his explorations into Central Africa from the east coast, a young man, **Fred Stanley Arnot**, who lived in Hamilton, during the time of Livingstone's visit, was greatly challenged by his report. He determined to bring the message of the gospel to the natives of Central Africa, approaching from the West coast and setting up mission stations, stretching right across from West to East.

Arnot had sailed to Africa in 1881, and for 7 years, travelled through Africa and starting out from what is now *Angola,* on the west coast of Central Africa, he and other two missionaries established a work in the interior in **Garenganze**, (currently known as **Katanga** - and I will in future refer to it by this name). Katanga is the most southern region of the country now known as the **D.R of Congo**. His short-term objective was to establish mission stations from the coast of Angola to Katanga.

Katanga was remote and difficult to reach from the coast but, regular supplies had to be provided for those working there, so that they could survive and trade.

In 1888, Arnot returned to Britain leaving behind, in Katanga, two fellow missionaries, Swan and Faulkner to cope on their own, while he brought to Britain the challenge to join them in his missionary work in Central Africa.

F.S. Arnot also had a strong association with the church/assembly at *Baillie's Causeway*, in Hamilton.

The Arnot family, including Fred's older brother William, was active there and, although the family moved back to Glasgow, before Fred became a missionary, such was their impact on the church, that one of the proposed new names for the church, when it moved to its new premises, in 1968, (now," *Selkirk Street Evangelical Church.,")* was *"Arnot Chapel"*.

Selkirk Street Evangelical Church is active today, in a modern building, among other Brethren churches in Hamilton. It has a continuing outstanding history of missionary activities. In 2008, it produced a history of its activities since its inception: *"40 YEARS OF WITNESS, Selkirk Street Evangelical Church Hamilton 1968-2008"*.

When F.S.Arnot visited Britain in 1888, to bring the challenge to other Christians to join in his work, he visited Hamilton and surrounding areas. **Daniel Crawford and Jeanie Gilchrist** responded to that challenge to join him, and other workers in Central Africa.

Daniel Crawford from Greenock, F.S. Arnot from Glasgow and Jeanie Gilchrist, formed the Scottish Brethren contingent, among missionaries from other countries, who departed with Arnot on the long voyage to the coast of Angola.

Records of the activities of Dan Crawford and F.S Arnot are still available: it is hoped that this book will revive interest in the contribution made by Jeanie Gilchrist.

The Christian Brethren's contribution to foreign missionary work in Central Africa, and in a number of countries, following on this initial work and during the twentieth Century has been truly remarkable!

The names, if not the stories, of the missionaries from the U.K., who are still in active service or listed as, "Senior and Retired Workers" are, as I write, in the *Echoes, Daily Prayer Guide 2010,* which I have before me. It begins with Africa – and the list is impressive. It does not contain names of those who have gone to be with the Lord – although some of those names bring back happy memories to older Christians, who came in contact with them and who will have lasting impressions of the dedication of these missionaries.

Some of those countries are today very troubled; especially the D.R of Congo, while others are still open to the gospel and this is reflected in the number and names of missionaries presently serving there.

**

Jeanie's *missionary travels, with illustrated maps.*
First, the maps!

I am delighted at having been able to produce two maps, which show for the first time, the extent of Jeanie's journeys by sea and land.

1. MAP 1 – is a modern map showing:

Her first and second voyages from London to Lisbon, in Portugal and then, on to Angola, on the West coast of Africa, arriving at the existing coastal town of Benguela.

The extent and direction of her *journeys inland*, reaching almost to the eastern border of Angola where it meets with the D.R of Congo. The (**2**) and (**3**) indicate the first and second focal points of her activities among the native women.

Her third voyage going directly from London – not via Lisbon, in Portugal and not this time, embarking on the West coast of Angola, - but proceeding down the West coast of Africa, then around the Southern coast of South Africa to approach her *intended* destination in D.R. of Congo, from the *East coast*, most likely stopping off at Biera, in Mozambique;

then we see her likely journey inward, from Beira. However, she was unable to continue on to her final destination: she died in Zambia before reaching it. She did however stop off at various places on the coast of South Africa before disembarking for her final journey inland.

Also marked on this map, is David Livingstone's final journey from the East coast, through Tanzania as far as Ujiji (not shown on the map), then turning south, and heading South West, as far as the Bengweulu Swamp, where he took seriously ill and returning to Ujiji. He died there.

I have shown Livingstone's final journey, for

completeness, as the map shows the progress made by the Scottish missionaries, mentioned earlier, to join West and East Central Africa with their mission stations. Other missionaries would come later to hugely expand the gospel outreach in this "*Beloved Strip*", by which name, it later became known.

One other important feature I have shown on the map, by means of a **black circle**, is the position of **Lake Mweru**. The Lake is too small to have been included on the original map. It forms part of the boundary between the D.R Congo and Zambia. Dan Crawford set up an important mission station on the west side of the lake, at Luanza, in the D.R of Congo.

2. MAP 2 – is a unique, more ancient map.
I came across it in my researches of this period of Jeanie's activities, relating to her first and second voyages and subsequent journeys inland, into the interior of Angola.

It is a *Wikipedia, free encyclopaedia map*, not produced for the purpose of showing the activities of missionaries: but to show the *chiefs and tribes* during the same period (dated 1880) and *the emergence of the main European colonial powers in this area*. It was coincidental that the missionaries happened to be evangelising the region at the same period, but invaluable to me in providing a fresh insight into the story of Jeanie's activities at that time. The map was produced in 2007.

Map 2, is a larger scale map than Map 1 and needs to be viewed alongside Map 1, which shows the African countries which now exist, but which didn't exist in the 1880's.

Of particular interest, are the Portuguese; Belgian (Leopold II) and British interests, clearly identified on Map 2.

It is of a sufficient scale, to show the position of Lake

Mweru, which I marked the position of, in Map 1. Ujiji is also shown, where David Livingstone died.

Dotted lines, on the map, indicate existing, trade routes, from Luanda and Benguela, in Angola. These routes go from the west coast to the east coast and would be a guide to the missionaries, as they journeyed inland, from Benguela.

I have marked (1) at the commencement of Jeanie's inward journey; (2) at her first stopping place (corresponding to my markings on Map 1), which was among the **Ovimbundu** tribe and (3) at her second, further inland, focal point of activities (again, as in Map 1).

Both maps should be followed closely in conjunction with the description of her journeys which follows.

** **

1. First Missionary Journey – 1889 -1894
Voyage by sea

JR's book gives the starting point as "spring", when F.S Arnot and his wife, accompanied by a party of outgoing missionaries left London for Central Africa, *via Lisbon*. Fred. Tatford, in his book, *Light over the Dark Continent,* mentions that it was a large party (no doubt with a good deal of luggage) and that there were in fact *two sailings* from Lisbon. The first party included the newly-wed Arnots, Dan Crawford and other named missionaries: the remainder of the party, including Jeanie, appear to have sailed from Lisbon on 22nd June. The first party arrived at Benguela, in Angola, on 9th May, so Jeanie would have arrived with the second party, sometime later – perhaps in early August.

JR mentions that there was "no direct route between Britain and Benguela". The reason for this, and why they had to sail from Lisbon, becomes clear from MAP 2. This shows that the Portuguese had a controlling interest at this time on the whole of the west coast of Angola: hence the need to sail from Lisbon on Jeanie's first two voyages.

Mention is made of the boat stopping off at various ports, including the Islands of Cape Verde and other small islands (off the coast of Mauritania), where the new missionaries saw, for the first time, the "*destitution*" of the native people.

At a number of these ports of call, a healthy, young, gifted and devout evangelist, from Ulster, Robert J Johnston, who was one of the most experienced evangelists among them, distributed tracts and as the steamer entered the Bay of Benguela, he suddenly "*passed into the presence of the Lord.*"

His sudden death was from fever, arising from the contacts he made at the various ports of call. On the very threshold of reaching the shores of Angola, his unexpected death, must have been a shock to his fellow missionaries. The news was flashed through the sea by cable, (a recent technological innovation) to the homeland: and Christians at home prayed earnestly for the safety of the other missionaries who had accompanied him.

Disease was to prove one of the greatest dangers faced by those early missionaries, who ventured forth into Central Africa.

On arrival at the coast, the two parties, now combined, had to begin their journey into the interior of Angola.

*Stage one, into the interior to the first base, at **Kuanjulula**, in Angola.*

Today, there is the famous Benguela railway but, in 1889, there were no roads or vehicles: the only way inland was by foot, along rough bridle paths – the trade routes – through "*a wild and mountainous country.*"As there were no recognised coins, the missionaries had to barter for food and other essentials and hire native carriers, mainly with their large supply of cloth, which they had brought along with them for this purpose.

F.S.Arnot had to go into the interior, before the second party of missionaries arrived, in order to hire native carriers. He succeeded in engaging 150 of them to transport the missionaries' luggage. This the carriers did by carrying the loads on their head and shoulders.

The size of the party, including the porters with their loads must have given Arnot, who was the party's leader some cause for concern. David Livingstone was able to explore new territories, because he always travelled with *as small a train* as possible, to avoid arousing suspicion among the natives and local tribal chiefs, who would be concerned about the purpose of such a large number: questions would arise in their minds as to whether they had guns or were slave traders.

Again, before they had progressed very far on their journey inland, four of the missionaries were struck down by an "epidemic of fever" – possibly malaria. Two of them, among the strongest and seemingly most healthy men, from England, died on 19th October 1889.

Sadly, one of those who died was Mr Morris, who had given up a lucrative position at home, and had come with his wife, leaving their four children at home. They intended bringing them to Africa later, once they themselves had settled there. Mrs Morris, suddenly finding herself so suddenly bereft of her husband, was forced to return home, accompanied by two others, to care for her now fatherless children.

JR mentions that the remainder of the party, including Jeanie, continued on their journey. He makes no mention of

Jeanie having suffered from this fever but, Fred Tatford, in his book, mentions, that Jeanie Gilchrist, was one of the four missionaries, who had suffered but, that she had recovered. If she was one of the sufferers, it would help explain why she suffered so much later due to illness.

These missionaries were pioneers, and among the first white people to venture into this area and, with little knowledge of the existence of tropical diseases, or of how to treat them, although some of the missionaries were medically trained, fevers were a constant danger which they had to face.

** **

Life in *Kuanjulula*

The surviving members from the two groups were reunited at Kuanjulula on 31st December 1889. Dan Crawford was one of those who welcomed the second group of missionaries on their arrival. He was one of the youngest of the missionaries, who had responded to F.S Arnot's earlier appeal.

The village of Kuanjulula does not appear on today's atlases but, I have indicated its approximate location with a (2) on both MAPS 1 and 2. It was near enough the coast for the Portuguese to have an influence there, as the local tribal chief, jealous of the missionaries' influence and stirred up by the Portuguese in the area, ordered them to leave the country: but, these Portuguese themselves were driven out. The Portuguese military, who came to investigate the cause, freed the missionaries from all suspicion of having caused trouble and allowed them to continue in peace, with their work of spreading the gospel.

While the main group of missionaries remained at Kuanjulula, three of the party, Thomson, Lane and Dan

Crawford continued with the convoy of carriers making for Bunkeya, the distant Capital of Katanga (Garenganze). This is shown on MAP 2, in the D.R of Congo, in chief **MSIRI's** (Misidi's) country. It was essential for them to go there to bring desperately needed supplies and relief to the two missionaries who had continued there, while Arnot had gone to Britain to seek for more missionaries to come and help in the work. Fred.Tatford, in his book, mentions that they arrived there on 7th November 1891 – which may be a misprint for 1890. On their arrival there, they found that Mr Faulkner had been ill for a year and it was essential for him to return home.

Kuanjulula was situated in the **OVIMBUNDU** (see Map 2). The people who lived in this fertile area were known as the **Umbundu**. Their warriors were active traders in slaves and commodities, trading these with the Portuguese at the coast. The Umbundu people were fairly numerous.

Jeanie remained in the area of Kuanjulula with other missionaries, for a year, learning the native Umbundu language and working among the women of the region: they were later joined by missionaries from other parts of the world. A knowledge of the Umbundu language would benefit Jeanie later, as she moved further into the interior, as the Umbundu often travelled inland to trade and used their language in communicating.

During Jeanie's time here, she and other missionaries established contacts with the various villages in the area.

JR's book has a picture of 11 missionaries, four of them women, who lived and worked together in the missionary compound in Kuanjulula. More substantial huts or houses were built there and fields and gardens planted in order to sustain them in their work.

A typical day in the life of Jeanie

JR gives a short description of the work Jeanie was engaged in during this time, which I have précised below.

Her day began at 5.30 or 6.00 am, when she would have a quiet time with the Lord then, after a meal, *girls* who were outcasts or rescued slaves, with sores or diseases seeking shelter and care, would gather round and listen to her stories of the Saviour.

Later, they would come to the "*school area,*" where they would sing hymns, learn Bible texts, join her in prayer and listen to her as she brought them God's message from the Bible, in their own language.

The women, worked hard all day in the fields and it was only in the evenings, that Jeanie was able to visit them *in their villages* and communicate with them as they sat in their simple, scarcely furnished, wood huts with grass roofs. All day long the women would be engaged is such activities as, sowing seed, grinding corn, hewing wood for the fires, and fetching water in pots: they carried the wood on their back and the water pots balanced on their head.

In the evening, Jeanie met with the women in their huts, as they pounded out their corn, or tended their children. She listened to their sad experiences; tended their sores and told them about the love of Jesus: "*She became their visitor, doctor, comforter and soul winner.*

Sometimes Jeanie suffered from fever, while she was unaccompanied, visiting women in their homes, and there, in most uncomfortable surroundings, she would have to suffer, seeking the Lord's help, until the fever left her.

Water for cooking, cleaning and washing was brought from the nearby river and food was brought in baskets by the natives, in the form of chicken, rice, fruit and vegetables, which the missionaries had to barter for in the form of cloth and beads.

Jeanie records the conversions of a young man and girl – Dick and Delunga – and their subsequent baptism in the local river, attended by a large group of interested spectators. They were later married and joined in the Christian fellowship.

**

Stage two, further into the interior to establish a new base at **Kavungu,** *in Angola.*
Having been joined by other missionaries, Mr Arnot decided to move further into the interior to establish a second base for missionary work, halfway between the west coast and the work in Bunkeya in Katanga. This base would also help to provide a vital link in transporting essential supplies and mail, from the homeland, to the workers in the interior. The new base would be in Kavungu.

In early August, 1891, a small company, including Jeanie, set forth, again with F.S.Arnot as their guide.

Little was known about the country ahead – whether the natives were hostile or friendly – there was the danger of wild animals and they had no defence or escorts. They depended on God alone to care for and protect them and to supply their needs. It was a true test of their faith.

Their aim was to move into the *"Lovale country,"* (the "Flats," a place of rivers and swamps) to a place, later identified as Kavungu, in Angola, on Angola's eastern border with DR Congo and Zambia. (See (**3**) marked on Maps 1 and 2).

Although Jeanie's heart was set on reaching the region *of Katanga* (Garenganze), Kavungu was the farthest point that

Jeanie reached in her first and second journeys into the interior from the west coast of Angola. (The "Multimap" of modern Angola shows townships of Kavungo and Lovua in this area of its map.)

Jeanie's diary of the long marches to Kavungu

Jeanie kept a diary of the journey inland. It covered the period from August 1st to October 15th – a period of *two and half-months*, which it took to complete the epic journey of some 500 miles, through difficult and dangerous territory.

Loads had to be prepared for the journey of the main party to Kavungu, and for the smaller group, which would continue much further on to Katanga (in the modern D.R of Congo) to provide supplies for the few missionaries who had advanced earlier into this area.

Jeanie describes this second base as, *"Na-Kandundu."* I later discovered that this was the name of the wife (Queen) of the tribal chief in the area, which is why it was not identifiable on today's atlas!

She records, at the beginning of her diary that news had just arrived of the death of a Mrs Sanders, whose husband was away at the west coast of Angola. What a shock he must have received, on his return to Kuanjulula, on finding his wife already dead and buried.

Jeanie mentions a number of contacts she had during the journey, as the convoy stopped at various villages, including one of the *"mother"* of a village, who took Jeanie to her house to ask why she had come. She explained to her and the large group of women and children, who had gathered to hear her, that she had come to bring the good news of Jesus and his love for them. Later, the woman returned to the travellers' camp and presented Jeanie with a chicken, a basket of corn, a pot of beans and two yams. In return Jeanie gave her two

71

handfuls of salt – which was to them, a great luxury. She also had regular contacts, during the long journey, with the girls who accompanied the porters.

The missionaries were also able to help those suffering with eye sores, applying ointments to help their recovery.

Mention is made in her diary of a number of river crossings on the journey and JR's book includes a picture of Jeanie being carried between two native carriers in a *"tipoia,"* resting and being sheltered from the sun. I wondered why she was not walking and there may have been a good reason, or perhaps it was because the culture was different then; but missionaries like the rest of us can have their weaknesses. On August 30th, they crossed the river Kuanza – the river *Cuanza* is clearly marked on modern atlases of Angola, where rivers are included.

Having reached the Lovale, or Flat country, Jeanie refers to long marches, through flat country, crossing many rivers and walking through marshes for hours on end. They pass *"many villages with no Christian witness"* and Jeanie pointedly remarks: *"What a fine field for some of the young men and women who are overcrowding the halls and treading on each other's heels at home!"*

Jeanie mentions the size of their convey, which included more than 250 carriers, following a flag, in a single line. This was significant larger than on their journey to the first base at Kuanjulula, when they had 150 carriers. She also records, that, on the same day, the party had covered a distance of 24 miles, *"and they all looked tired."*

On 15th October they arrived at their destination, in Kavungu. Mr Thompson continued on, with some of the carriers, to deliver letters and supplies to Dan Crawford and Lane in Katanga, in D.R.of Congo.

By this time, the work was expanding at the mission station in Kuanjulula and a picture is shown in JR's book, of a large, substantial, Day School in the missionary compound there, with around 80 to 100 pupils and teachers, positioned in the front of the building.

Life in **Kavungu**

When the missionaries arrive at **Kavungu,** they notice a large number of native huts in the main *"Capital"* of the area.

The queen earlier referred to by Jeanie as **Na-Kandundu** is introduced to the missionaries by Mr Arnot – who had already met her on a previous visit to the area. The small group of missionaries included two married couples and Jeanie. Arnot explained to the queen that they desired to set up a mission station in the area. The ageing Queen agreed to the request and presents were exchanged.

As Mr and Mrs Arnot were about to return to Kuanjulula , the Queen presented Mr Arnot with an ox , requiring him to shoot it, while she and her husband placed their hands on his shoulders. It was a local custom, partly designed as a mark of friendship and partly expressing her wish that no harm would come to the missionaries, as they built their station among her people.

Shortly after this event, for three months of the wet season, which followed, the missionaries camped under an old oak tree and a smallpox epidemic caused the death of a number of Africans in the area. This created difficulties for the missionaries, as many of the Africans refused to sell them any food, attempting to starve them out. But, God brought them through these difficulties; buildings were erected and a mission station established.

Jeanie had a substantial house built and worked there, alongside the other missionaries for two years.

When the Arnots returned to Kuanjulula, Fred was so ill that his fellow missionaries insisted that he and his wife return home for a time of recuperation, which they reluctantly did in 1892.

A second mission station had now been established, as the missionaries progressed from west to east: a third base was also under way in Bunkeya, in the Katanga region of D.R of Congo, through the efforts of the few pioneers who had already gone there.

Meeting the slave trade

I have already mentioned the high incidence of recurring fevers affecting the missionaries and of outbreaks of smallpox among the African natives but, another matter of great concern to the missionaries was the traffic in African slaves by Arab and African traders, which blighted the lives of so many of the African people.

During her stay at Kavungu, Jeanie tells of the heartbreaking sight of seeing as many as 800 slaves being marched along those routes, *"including men women and children, mothers with babies, strong young women and men carrying loads and little children scarcely able to walk, some not more than four years old. The weak if they were unable to continue were beaten with clubs by their cruel masters or left to die by the wayside."*

She also recounts how at the mission station in Kavungu, a little daughter of *MSIRI* (Misidi), the powerful tribal chief,(see MAP 2), whose name was *Mwewa* , was being cared for by the missionaries, subsequent to the murder of MSIRI.

Mwewa's mother had fled with her daughter and while working in a village field in her own area of Lamba, one of the villagers had stolen Mwewa and sold her to one of the Umbundu warriors (see Ovimbundu in MAP 2), in west

Angola. On the long journey to the west, her master had forced her to carry two heavy elephant tusks, during long marches and had whipped her along the path as far as Kavungu. As they reached there, the little girl could walk no further because of large sores on her legs.

Her owner approached the missionaries and asked for medicine to cure her. They refused, but offered to redeem and care for her. He agreed to this for the price of twenty yards of cloth and a red handkerchief.

After two years service at Kavungu, Jeanie's health began to deteriorate and it was decided that she needed a change. She did not improve on the long journey to the coast and was taken by steamer to reach England on New Year's Day, **1894.**

**

2. Fourteen months recuperation in Great Britain
A few comments from Jeanie's diary during this period were of particular interest to me. I note these below.

With the help of other Christians who cared for her at this time, she was able to visit "*the battlefield of Drumclog, where Claverhouse attacked the Covenanters on Sunday, in June 1679. We are now enjoying in peace what our forefathers had to fight for.*"

She also "*visited Chapelton, Larkhall and Hamilton, bringing early memories to mind,*" there she was renewed and encouraged by meeting former friends.

And, "*she visited Bristol and had a deeply interesting conversation with the patriarchal George Muller*"; and she paid a visit to "*Barnstaple, enjoying godly fellowship and profiting by the spiritual ministry of the aged Robert C Chapman, in his 93rd year, full of heavenly joy...*"

As a young man, I was deeply influenced, as many others have been, by reading about George Muller, who by faith alone, ran an orphan home for a great many homeless children and received many answers to prayer; and by the gracious, Christ-like behaviour of R.C. Chapman, one of the early members of the Christian Brethren. What a thrill it must have been for Jeanie to meet these two men in the twilight of their lives and receive encouragement from them.

It is not surprising that we then read, "*Health being restored, and the way made clear, she began to get ready to return to Africa in the spring of 1895*"...

3. Second Missionary Journey – 1895 – 1897.
This time Jeanie did not go out with a large missionary party, but was accompanied by two ladies. They left for Benguela on 8th April 1895, on the same route as before, via Lisbon, arriving at **Kuanjulula** on 22nd June, some two and a half months later.(see her destination marked by a (**2**) on MAPs 1 and 2.)

JR records that, while Jeanie was recovering at home, a further mission base had been opened at **Luanza, on Lake Mweru.** (See the position of the Lake on MAP 2 and my identification of its position on MAP 1). I could not identify the place name, Luanza, but the river Luanza converges with Lake Mweru at its north-west side. Dan Crawford established a mission station there and he and his companions experienced great blessing.

As MAP 2 shows, progress to the Lake was a further step in linking up mission stations from the west coast of Angola to the east coast of Tanzania, as ultimately planned by F.S Arnot. But this station may have resulted from events following on the murder of Chief MSIRI, which I will explain later. Nevertheless, as MAPs 1 and 2 show, the journeys of David Livingstone from the east and the other named missionaries from the west had now almost been connected, leaving only the gap between Lake Mweru and Lake Tanganyika!

So far, I have indicated that Jeanie had reached Kuanjulula on her second journey after arriving at Benguela, in Angola. It is not clear to me from JR's Book, whether she ever reached further, into Kavungu (marked (3) on my maps.). On balance, I do not think she was able to advance further, being prevented from doing so by poor health.

Great blessing appears to have accompanied the initial work of the pioneers in Kuanjulula, with a number of the natives converting and places of worship and witness being set up in the area. Jeanie's help was greatly appreciated, as she fitted into the spheres of activity, which she had engaged in on her first journey there.

JR mentions the names of a significant number of the original pioneer missionaries, who had worked in Kuanjulula and Kavungu, who had by now suffered ill-health and been forced to return home or had died in service. One of the workers had died as a result of a bite from a mad dog.

But, despite the savage toll, the work was progressing in these areas and would continue to expand rapidly. Medical advances would enable future missionaries to expand the work, while suffering less from fevers and native workers would play an important role in the years which lay ahead.

JR ends this phase of Jeanie's work with the following delightful story.

Pokanwa was employed by an Arab slave trader and was a strict Muslim. During a time of conflict, he found sanctuary in the missionaries' compound in Katanga and made his way to Kavungu. For a long time, he clung to his religion but he became a Christian and was baptised. *Mwewe*, who I mentioned earlier, was the daughter of the tribal chief MSIRI, and after MSIRI was murdered, she became a slave girl and was rescued by the missionaries in Kavungu.

By the time *Pokanawa* arrived there, *Mwewe* too had become a Christian and was now a grown woman living with the missionaries. The happy ending to the story is that *Pokanaw*a, the slave trader's assistant, married, *Mwewe*, the slave girl: the grace of God had united the apparently irreconcilable.

Jeanie's health again affected her to such an extent that she was forced to return home some time in 1897.

**

Interlude – *My observations and perspective on the effects of political changes, as viewed from the year 2010.*
Modern research and advances in technology since the 1890's and the passage of time since then, enables us to view the work of these pioneer missionaries in Angola and in D.R. Congo in the wider context of political events in the 1890's and later.

Central Africa was then only beginning to be explored; the interior was largely unknown and maps of that time bear little or no resemblance to today's atlases of the same area. This reflects the huge changes which have taken place and are still taking place in Africa. Events were recorded, as in JR's Book, largely through the eyes of the individual missionaries of that period.

MAP 2, produced in 2007, shows the major tribal chieftains and their territories, in the 1880's, - some of whom are referred to in JR's Book - and the early advances of European colonial interests, which were later to change the face of the whole of Africa from 1891 to the 1920's. The European countries shown on MAP 2 are Britain, Portugal and Belgium.

The map shows what Central Africa would have looked like during the times of Jeanie's visits in the 1890's.

MAP 1, shows the changed face of Africa, as it is today: the whole of Africa was divided into separate countries by 1914, each being controlled by a European power and many of these countries have been the subject of further huge changes, in the much troubled Continent, to produce the map as it is today. These changes had a significant bearing on the new direction taken by Jeanie on her third and final voyage.

The slave trade

Prior to Jeanie's arrival, -from the 16th to the early 19th Century - Luanda and Benguela, in Angola, were the main ports for transporting African slaves to the America's, including the US, and it is estimated that the Portuguese took over 7 million slaves from Angola, via the Atlantic Slave Trade, during this period. Slaves were supplied with the support of the Umbundu warriors, in exchange for guns and European goods. Portuguese authorities abolished slavery in 1836 but it continued much later and between 1808 and 1860, the British navy, intent on abolishing the slave trade in the seas, seized 1600 vessels transporting slaves. By 1860, trade in Angola's *West coast* was largely based on exploiting Angola's agricultural resources. But the slave trade and slavery continued in the interior into the early part of the 20th Century.

The Arabs, on the *East coast*, controlled the transporting of slaves and spices, via the coast of Tanzania and Zanzibar through the Indian Ocean, to Europe and India. From the 12th – 20th Century, it is estimated that some 18 million slaves had been taken. By the late 19th Century, the British navy had blocked off the trade in slaves by sea.

David Livingstone in his final explorations into the interior from Zanzibar had been appalled by the killings and cruelty he had witnessed. On one occasions he witnessed a large number of unsuspecting African men, women and children, being shot by Arab traders in Lake Tanganyika and he reported that the steamer's paddles could hardly turn because the bodies of dead black slaves in the lake were clogging up the paddles.

Livingstone's appeal to the British government to stop the slave trade via the East coast was one of the contributory factors to the British navy sending its ships to patrol the coast of Tanzania, thus preventing the Arabs from shipping slaves any more by sea.

The slave trade continued in the Interior of East Central Africa, however, and **Tippu Tip** (see MAP2) became known as the last and greatest of the Zanzibar traders of the 19th Century. In seeking to expand his empire in the 1880's he burned villages, killing the people and floating their bodies in the river and had 2300 slaves in chains ready to force them on the long journey to the markets of Zanzibar.

This was the background to Jeanie's recorded experiences of the slave trade.

But other great events were about to take place following on the arrival of Jeanie and the other missionaries in 1890.

European colonisation of Africa

While the missionaries were independently seeking to advance the *spiritual kingdom of Christ* other forces were at work, as the major European countries, already extending their empire by sea, turned their attention to the great natural resources of Africa. European countries were about to advance their *material kingdoms* and absorb Africa into their Empires.

MAP 2, is a picture of the situation in the *1880's,* showing not only the substantial influence and power of the tribal chiefs, but that European countries were beginning to exert their influence - albeit with the initial support of the tribal chiefs.

MAP 1, shows part of Africa, divided into different countries, including Central Africa, and although this is a current map of Africa, within the space of 40 years, by 1920, all the countries in Africa were already in existence, with their boundaries largely determined - only, they were not *independent countries* as they are today - but each was part of a *colonial empire.*

The arrival of the missionaries, in the interior, including Jeanie, in 1891 coincided with a key event, which would ignite these great changes.

JR in his book, in relating the story of Jeanie's first journey inland, also records that Dan Crawford and a small group continued on to *Katanga in D.R of Congo* to bring supplies to the small group of missionaries already there. In this connection he mentions MSIRI, the tribal chief of this region, who was known to the two or three missionaries who were there. JR then mentions the killing of MSIRI, as follows, "*in his old age, his power was being threatened by the Belgians ... .several of his unwilling subjects had risen against him.. A young officer shot him .. **and a European Protectorate has made it impossible for another despot to arise**".* We might have made a similar comment had we been writing at that time! But, now, more than a century later, with hindsight, and with a greater knowledge of the circumstances in which MSIRI was killed and of subsequent events, I can briefly offer a different perspective on MSIRI's killing.

Looking at MAP 2, we can see that while Portugal had control of the Coast of Angola, the rather, recently emerged, weaker nation of Belgium had power over the area around the River Congo referred to as the Congo Free State. This was under the control of **Leopold (II)**, who was the titular king of Belgium.

When **Henry Morton Stanley** returned to Britain and Europe after meeting David Livingstone and reporting that he was still alive, he sought to interest the decision makers in Europe in the untapped resources of Central Africa. As most of the European countries were already active in expanding their empires elsewhere, only one person appears to have responded – Leopold II.

In 1883, using Stanley's skills and knowledge of the tribes in Central Africa, Leopold set about carving out for *himself* the whole of what is now known as **D.R Congo**.

The king's story is one of intrigue, cruelty and manipulation which beggars belief. He used deceit in pretending to be against slavery, which was being abolished, but replaced this by a tyranny of *enforced labour* and land grabbing, on a scale never before witnessed in Africa.

As I write this section in 2010, the developed countries of the world are presently suffering from a near collapse of their economies, caused mainly by the irresponsible, selfish actions of leaders of some major western banks. Many ordinary working people have suffered as a consequence, and many cases of major fraud have been revealed. Their forerunner was King Leopold II - and in terms of the suffering he imposed he made chief MSIRI look like an amateur!

Leopold's was the first of the "*European Protectorates*". The colonial "explorers" would become exploiters, exploiting the resources of Africa for their own enrichment; the "Protectorates" would largely protect their own interests; the horrors of slavery would be replaced by the tyranny of enforced labour – and this had nothing to do with our missionaries!

Some colonial powers were more benevolent than others and sought to educate and improve the conditions of the people they administered. When eventually each country received its independence, it was sadly, often the case that the colonial powers were replaced by autocratic native dictators, - as is currently the case in Zimbabwe - who have brought great suffering, starvation and impoverishment to the ordinary people, who are seeking to oppose their dictatorial rule.

Coming back to *Katanga*, Cecil Rhodes realising the material wealth and resources of this region, sent an expedition to MSIRI offering to buy Katanga from him, at the same time as Dan Crawford had arrived in the area to provide relief to the small number of missionaries there. It was 1891.

The tribal chief, MSIRI turned down the British approach and King Leopold sent four unsuccessful expeditions to him and when the last, powerful military expedition arrived, MSIRI was shot and a more conciliatory chief put in his place: the whole of Katanga came under the control of Leopold II, in Belgium.

Leopold, succeeded in acquiring and subduing the remaining regions to form what is now know as the D.R of Congo, a vast area. In the process he employed the organisational and negotiating skills of H.M Stanley, to achieve his objectives. Enforced native labour was used to open up the country and provide cheap labour to exploit the regions resources, including rubber plantations and as the sole beneficiary, he became exceedingly wealthy.

The actions and methods used by Leopold was one of a number of reasons for the substantial reduction in the population of the D.R of Congo during the period of his administration. The disaster was ultimately exposed and the territory was taken from him and given to the Belgian Government in 1908, when it became known as the *Belgian Congo*.

This country like much of Africa, has suffered greatly from internal conflict and exploitation and even today, it is a troubled country.

One of the British Protectorates in Africa was *Rhodesia*, which is now divided into two countries, Zimbabwe and Zambia.

Christian Brethren missionaries have been active in all the countries of Central Africa in the 20th Century and are still active in some today. Often the current presence of missionaries in the various countries of Central Africa, during a particular period, is a useful guide to the freedom being enjoyed in that country at the time.

Today, another power is making inroads into Africa – China, with its great wealth, is making its influence felt in a number of countries including Zambia and Angola. Oil exploration companies are also making an impact on countries in Central Africa; who knows what effects the recent discovery of oil by an outside Company, on the Uganda side of Lake Albert will have on the ordinary people of Uganda, whose average life span is forty years.

One might well ask what role the Christian Brethren missionaries have played in relation to these events in Central Africa.

The answer is that while Dan Crawford and other missionaries were involved in missionary outreach in Katanga, it is widely acknowledged, that they played no part in the political situation that surrounded the death of MSIRI, but remained neutral to the political forces.

Theirs was a spiritual mission, to save souls and change lives and to educate and improve the health and welfare of the Africans.

As a result of their sacrificial efforts, throughout the "Beloved Strip," they have seen many turning to the Lord; local churches have been set up for worship and witness with their own native evangelists and elders, and these have multiplied throughout the regions. They have given hope and love to a suffering people.

One of the more immediate effects of the death of MSIRI and the subsequent turmoil in Katanga was that the missionaries lives were endangered and Dan Crawford and some others appear to have moved eastward to set up a missionary station at Luanza, on the DR Congo side, of Lake Mweru. This work greatly prospered and has been richly blessed.

**

4. Six years recovering and preparing to return once more to Africa

JR does not mention the date when Jeanie left Africa to return home, but he does mention her absence for six years before embarking again on her final voyage to Africa *on 23rd May 1903*. Her absence must have covered the years from 1897 to early 1903.

During those years, Jeanie spent a good deal of time in Germany, where her treatment involved, "*a course of baths.*" There she was accompanied by a Jeanie Prentice, who also was of a mind to go to Africa.

On her recovery, she received repeated requests from Christians in US and Canada, to visit them and tell of her work. Three of the first missionaries, who had gone to serve the Lord in Central Africa, William Faulkner, and Mr and Mrs Bird, had gone from Canada and on the death of Mr Bird, Mrs Bird was living in America. Christian Brethren Assemblies/Churches in Canada and US were greatly interested in the work in Central Africa and Jeanie in response to their requests, sailed for Boston, on 13th February 1901.

She spent the best part of a year visiting Canada and US, giving a report of her work at *Women's Report Meetings* and stirring up an interest in the work in Central Africa, challenging others to become involved. Quite a number of the women were making garments for the missionaries and natives in Africa and she encouraged them in this work.

In January 1902, she left New York to visit the West Indies, as a number of missionaries had gone out to the work from some of these islands.

Feeling strengthened in health and spirit Jeanie prepared once more to return to the Continent, where her heart lay. She returned to Britain and after making visits to relatives and friends in Scotland and England, she departed for Africa.

5. Third and final Missionary Journey – 1903

On Saturday, *May 23rd 1903*, Jeanie set sail from Southampton. Her heart was set, as before, in serving her Lord, in the *Katanga Province, (Garenganze)*, in the D.R of Congo: this she had been unable to achieve on her first two journeys.

In my "*Interlude,*" I explained some of the great changes which were taking place, largely as a result of the European colonisation of Central Africa. Now, on her third voyage, Jeanie no longer had to sail *via Lisbon*, to the *west coast of Angola*, on a Portuguese vessel, and proceed on the long journey inland, as before. Now, she was able to sail direct on a *British* ship from Southampton, - as I shall now explain - via *Mozambique*, on the *East* coast of Africa.

She travelled by boat, down the whole of the west Coast of Africa, around the south coast and attempted the journey inland from the *East* Coast. (See MAP 1, where I have marked out her **third** voyage and attempted journey inland.)

My approximate calculations show that Jeanie must have travelled around 6400 miles by sea on each of her first two journeys, then inland on foot another 500 miles or more. On her final journey she would travel around 9800 by sea followed by another 500 miles inland.

** **

JR mentions that Jeanie intended joining the new mission station at Koni Hill (Koni?), where a number of brethren were working including John Clark, who had arranged to come and meet her. Three stations had now been established in the interior: *"Johnston Falls, Koni Hill and Luanza, several days apart, as at the three points of a triangle."*

I have now been able to identify Johnston Falls as being *Mambilima Falls*, just inside the border of Zambia, with the D.R of Congo to its immediate north; *Luanza* I have already mentioned was Dan Crawford's station, which I have shown on MAP1 as being on the north west side of Lake Mweru and Koni Hill is perhaps *Koni*, (west of Luanza).Both *Luanza and Koni* were in the southern part of the D.R of Congo.

JR gives a brief account of Jeanie's journey by sea.

A modern map of South Africa will identify most of the places where she stopped off on reaching the southernmost point of South Africa.

She embarked for some time at *Cape Town* on the west, meeting and encouraging Christian workers there. While there, she visited *Robben Island, the Leper settlement* and was deeply moved by the sight of their disfigurement and suffering. She tells of two lepers, *"with their heads completely bandaged, with only two little holes for their eyes to look through and the same for their mouth to receive food."*

On 2nd July, she sailed for *Durban*, -on the East coast of South Africa - calling in at a number of places on the way, including *Port Elizabeth*,(on the south coast) and *East London*, (as you turn on to the east coast) to meet with and encourage the Christian fellowships there.

When the ship arriving at *Durban*, she was able to bring news from relatives at home to isolated friends there. She also received news that John Clark who was to meet her on her final journey inland was *"severely ill from fever, and had been advised by the doctor to go to South Africa to recuperate, but as the season was well advanced and she had not received any word from him, she decided to press on."* One can scarcely imagine, what a lonely and difficult decision Jeanie had to make and how sure her faith in God must have been, in such trying circumstances.

On 10th August, she sailed from Durban heading up the east coast and arrived at a place called **Chinde** on 23rd August, exactly three months after leaving Southampton.

I had not been able to find where **Chinde** was but Jean Kruse, retired missionary from Zambia had suggested to me, when I set out to research Jeanie's story that Jeanie may have headed inland from **Beira** in **Mozambique** (see MAP 1). My researches would suggest that Jean Kruse was correct and that it was certainly in this area that Jeanie disembarked.

JR's book mentions that the remainder of her journey was by a small river steamer, with a large barge at each side full of natives and cargo and that the captain halted for half-an-hour at *Shupenga* to give the opportunity to visit the grave of Mrs David Livingstone, (the eldest daughter of Robert Moffat,the pioneer missionary to South Africa) who died at the early age of 41. Worldwide Missions' comments on Mary Livingstone indicate that, *"she went to her grave by the great Zambesi,"* and Livingstone himself wrote, *"Poor Mary lies on Shupanga brae."*

Two of the great African rivers reach the coast of Mozambique, one at the south, the Limpopo River, and the other in the proximity of Beira, the **Zambezi** River. The latter is the fifth largest river in the world, crossing a number of the countries in Central Africa.It has been dammed in a number of places and its impressive delta is reckoned to be only half the size it was in Jeanie's time. In the year 2000, Mozambique suffered one of its worst experiences of flooding.

At this point in my researches, I unexpectedly came across a recent single, entry in *Wikipedia* relating to Mozambique, it reads as follows: *"The Chinde River is a distributary of the Zambezi river delta in Mozambique and the town of **Chinde** is located on its bank."* I am now certain this is the river JR was referring to, which Jeanie travelled on, as she began her journey inward from the coast of Mozambique heading for Koni in D.R of Congo.

Jeanie had received a number of letters from missionaries serving in Africa, encouraging her on, on her journey and assuring her of a warm welcome. These included a letter from Luanza and another saying: *"Welcome to Garenganze."* Dan Crawford had telegraphed her from Blantyre in Malawi, where he was at that time engaged in printing the New Testament in the native language –clearly technology had greatly improved communications, since her last visit!

John Clark had come to the coast to meet her and the two had travelled inland on the long journey to her desired destination in Katanga; but like a sad human ending to a wonderful story, it was not to be - but God had called her up higher to be with Himself.

They had reached as far as *Fort Jameson*, which I am informed is now **Chipata,** shown on recent maps as being the border post between Zambia and Malawi: there, loads and carriers had been arranged, in preparation for the final part of her journey.

But, in her endeavours to assist in the preparations, she had overworked in the sun. A week later, when on their journey, *"fifty miles north-west of Chipata, she had a sharp attack of fever; her temperature rising to 106 degrees."* Although she improved the following day, in the evening, she slipped into unconsciousness and *"passed away to be with the Lord, from the midst of the African forest"*. Based on my calculations, she was 50 years old.

The story of this Chapelton lass, reveals a woman of great devotion, courage and self-sacrifice. For Jeanie, no sacrifice was too great in the cause of spreading the gospel of Christ and caring for others. She had the unique honour of being the first Scottish lady missionary to join with the male members of Stanley Arnot's team to spread the good news of the gospel to the primitive tribes of Central Africa.

She experienced great hardship on the long, arduous journey in a steamboat from London to Africa – seeking even then to care for others who were ill on the journey. In her travels with the team into the interior of Africa, and while living there, she faced the dangers and difficulties of a hostile environment; of attack from wild beasts; of hostility from warring tribes and often being laid low by unknown fevers and diseases in the most primitive of conditions, which were foreign to anything she had ever experienced before.

She could echo the words of Paul *"I have fought a good fight, I have finished my course, I have kept the faith."* and as assuredly, she would hear the words of the Master, she served so well: *"Well done! Good and faithful servant"* and receive her due reward.

Eternity alone will reveal the achievements of this remarkable woman who laid her life on the altar for God. May her story be a challenge and an encouragement to all who seek to serve the Lord.

**

Jeanie's influence, a century on!

As I indicated earlier, two recent contacts have added fresh light and interest to JR's story of Jeanie written around 1910.

Jack and Frances Martin

Jack, and his daughter Frances, are direct descendants of James Gilchrist of Chapelton, on Jack's mother's side.

Frances was tracing back her family tree on the Gilchrist line and when Jack contacted me, she was able to provide me with Jeanie's missing year of birth, which enabled me to determine what age she was at the critical points in her life and how old she was when she died.

How thrilling to learn that Frances, who is the fifth generation from James Gilchrist – Jeanie was her great, great Aunt – living more than 135 years after James's decease, still shares the same faith as her forebear, James Gilchrist of Chapelton.

They also provided me with some helpful photographs.

The *first*, shows the **James Gilchrist**, of Chapelton, - the first available picture, I believe, of this remarkable man. He is first on the left of the picture (see page 52).

The *second,* shows **Jeanie**, his daughter, among the workers in the Gilchrist bakery in Hamilton. She is first on the left of the picture (see page 55).

The history of the Gilchrist bakery is interesting. From James Gilchrist the baker in Chapelton, we can trace, through the 1891, 1894 and 1895 Census, the establishment of the bakery business in *24, 26, 28 Woodside Walk, Hamilton*, where Jeanie resided. It was commonly known as: *"The Gilchrist Building."* Later, the Company expanded to Ayrshire and grew to become a substantial business in Prestwick and Ayr.

In Ayr, it was known as the: *"Land o' Burn's"* bakery", which included a shop and restaurant complex. Today the site, where it once existed, is occupied by a large car park just behind the main, central Bus Station. It seems that God prospered the Gilchrist family, both materially and spiritually, in the years which followed the conversion of James Gilchrist.

It was the grandson of the baker in Chapelton, and Jeanie's nephew whose name also was '*James Gilchrist*', who established the bakery in Ayr.

The following narrative appeared in the Ayrshire Post in 2006 relating to a visit by this nephew, "50 years ago," in **1956** to Jeanie's burial place, in Zambia.

At the age of 72, he fulfilled his boyhood vision of visiting the place where Jeanie was buried in Rhodesia. He travelled by plane, truck and on foot to the grave, which had a wooden board stating, "In memory of Jeanie Gilchrist, missionary on her way to Koni Hill, Garanganze, who fell asleep in Jesus, 17th November 1903 - faithful unto death." Her grave had been tended by native people.

Jeanie Gilchrist plaque erected in 1956 by her nephew James Gilchrist.

James arranged for a concrete slab, with a bronze plaque to mark Jeanie's resting place. The *third* photograph bears the inscription on the plaque and a picture of Jeanie.

It has also been an exciting adventure for me, as I have sought diligently to research the Jeanie's story and bring it to life once more for the current generation to enjoy.

Agnes Hislop, Selkirk Evangelical Church, Hamilton.
I was already aware of Jeanie's background in Hamilton and her association with Selkirk Evangelical Church and one evening, in Woodpark Evangelical Church, Ayr, where I am currently a member, when we were celebrating the joint 90th birthdays' of a lovely Christian couple, Angus

and Jenny MacLeod, I was seated beside Agnes Hislop. I mentioned to her that I was in the process of writing a book about Chapelton, (that was three years ago!) which would include the story of Jeanie Gilchrist. She related to me, and later e-mailed me, this fascinating story about Jeanie. (Agnes, as I have already mentioned, was a Christian Brethren missionary for many years in Pakistan.)

It was about Agnes's encounter with a patient in the Southern General Hospital, Glasgow around 1950-51. Here are Agnes's own words, describing her experience:

"When I was doing "relief" night duty in hospital work, I was sent to whichever ward needed a replacement for a nurse's night off.

One night, when I went on duty, a young couple were standing in the corridor. They informed me that they had been called by the hospital, as his mother was seriously ill and in a coma. Later, they decided to leave, and after I had made them a cup of tea, I promised I would call them if there was any further change in his mother's condition.

In the morning, the old lady was still lying in a coma and I decided to freshen her up with a wash and comb her hair. As I washed her face, she opened her eyes. I told her that her son and his wife had been so see her and had told me she lived in Hamilton, (where I lived, at that time,) and that she was a contemporary of Harry Lauder's. She replied, "No' me, hen!" She told me she had lived in Hamilton, when she was young, and that her house had been above the "Gilchrist bakers" and that Jeanie Gilchrist had been her Sunday school teacher. On asking her which Sunday school she had attended, she replied "Baillie's Causeway", which is the place where I was in fellowship at that time.

I then asked her if she had ever trusted the Saviour Jeanie Gilchrist had told her about. She replied "No, hen, but that is what I am thinking about in these days." (Amazing that, while she was unconscious, this is what she was thinking about). I asked her if she would like to trust Him and she said a definite "yes". We prayed together and she trusted the Lord.

Before I went off duty she slipped again into a coma and died two days later.

As the years have passed I have been more and more struck by the ways of God in this."

The story of Jeanie Gilchrist did not end when she died in Zambia.

**

PART THREE
Kinnaird's Childrens Work in Chapelton Village

(Thirty eight years work among Chapelton village children - 1967-2004: the work of Martha and David Kinnaird and their team of helpers.)

David's conversion

When David was a young teenager, living in the town of Strathaven, he went through a prolonged period of trying circumstances in his home and decided to leave. He went to live with his Uncle and Aunt in their manse, in the town of Arbroath, on the east coast of central Scotland. His uncle was the *"Session Church Minister."*

During David's stay there, the Arbroath Mission had decided to organise a gospel outreach effort and had engaged Brigadier General Frost to lead it (subsequently referred to as BG Frost). Part of the mission included holding outside services in the streets of Arbroath.

On one particular wet and windy evening, the team discussed among themselves whether or not to hold a street service that night. BG Frost was in favour of going ahead arguing that, "there might be one person in need of salvation who might hear and respond to God's message, despite the inclement weather." His view was accepted.

That night, after a hymn and prayer, BG Frost preached his message.

It was based on the well-known Bible verse, (Revelation Chapter 3, verse 20.) *"Behold I stand at the door and knock. If any man hear my voice and open the door I will come in...."* The team went home that evening, after the short service in the street; unaware that one person "in need" had heard the verse – David Kinnaird!

When David set out that wild autumn night he wasn't remotely interested in the God of the Bible or of the relevance of God's Word to his life! Instead, he had been drinking brandy in a local pub, and being drunk, had fallen into the roadside gutter and lay there unnoticed during the service.

But God was at work and when David came to, he made his way home to his uncle's house; the words of the text and their relevance to his own circumstances were brought home to him with great conviction by the Holy Spirit. Two weeks later, he went to visit BG Frost in his caravan, where the evangelist stayed during his Mission.

There, in the caravan David accepted Jesus as his personal Saviour and receiving God's forgiveness, became a Christian: David was 19 years of age.

Some time later, he decided to return to his home town of Strathaven, where he was able to find shared, rental accommodation. While living there, David decided to attend the services of the Strathaven Gospel Hall in Lethame Road. Shortly after, he was baptised by immersion and became a member of the church.

At this time I was living in Glassford and was a member of the *"Shiloh Hall"* Christian Brethren assembly there. I was responsible for the Bible Classes both in Strathaven and Glassford. These were well attended by young people and David attended the one in Strathaven, where he was enthusiastic in his service for God. He had few of this world's possessions and as he approached his 21st birthday, the members of the Strathaven Bible Class, decided to buy him a suit of clothes.

At that time, I was courting Ann Jack, who later became my wife. Ann's father was a hill farmer living at Hall of Kype farm, near Sandford, some three miles outside of Strathaven. For many years he and his family and helpers had a large Sunday school in Sandford village hall, which was attended by most of the village children. We arranged a special party at the farm to celebrate David's 21st birthday and to present him with his new suit of clothes.

David's marriage to Martha Moore and their move to Chapelton.
After the events just recorded, David became a member of the Glassford Shiloh Hall. There he met Martha Moore, who was a member. They were married on 14th November1963.

Martha's father, John Moore, was an elder in the *Shiloh Hall*. He was greatly interested in foreign missionary work. Although the church membership was small - around 30 - it became an active centre for missionary interest and over the years, a number of the Moore family, and other members, became missionaries.

John Moore's eldest son Alex courted Mary Cummings (a convert from the village at around the same time as me). Both went out as missionaries to Pakistan, where they married. Alex died shortly after, in Pakistan at the age of 24. Mary, his wife, continued there, for 18 years. Alex's younger sister Elsie, also served God in Pakistan for 30 years, until her retirement.

But this part of the story centres on the activities of Martha and David in the village of Chapelton.

After their marriage, they lived in temporary accommodation in Glassford. They looked for a suitable house, in Glassford, but couldn't find one. Later, when Martha was expecting their second child, the situation became more urgent. They heard that a wooden house was for sale in the neighbouring village of Chapelton, at 40 Shawton Road, were successful in buying it and moved to their new home in Chapelton, in April 1966. Both of them were in their thirties.

Shortly after their arrival, they became friends with two elderly sisters, Isa and Alice Hood, who were members of the *Seamen's Mission*. The sisters told them that they had been praying for a number of years that God would send a young couple to live in Chapelton and start a work for God there. David and Martha were encouraged and challenged by this news.

A girl's class, for ages 9 and over is started at 40 Shawton Road. (1967-1969)

In the spring of 1967, Martha started a children's work in their home on Sunday and Wednesday evenings. She befriended the children; was a ready listener and through God's Word, showed them His way of salvation. Around twelve children attended regularly and some accepted Jesus as their Saviour, during this time.

One of the outstanding contacts they made, during this period was with a girl whose name was Marian Morrison. She later studied medicine and became a doctor. Marian believed that God was calling her to use her professional skills as a Christian missionary.

During her "Year Out," Marian spent three months in India, with the *Leprosy Mission*. Her more permanent call came when she went out with *Interserve* to Pakistan, where she has worked for almost twenty years in the *Women's Christian Hospital* in Multan.(Martha's younger sister, Elsie also worked there). She also played an important role in negotiations with Government officials regarding the provision of Medical Services in a wider area in Pakistan.

In the summer of 1969, the *Lanarkshire Gospel Work* (LGW) decided to erect their portable tent in the field opposite the Kinnaird's home and they held services there for adults and children. *Harold German* was the evangelist responsible for this short-term summer work.

One morning, around 5.00am, the roof of the portable Hall was blown off in a very high wind. It struck and shattered the Kinnaird's front sitting room window. This incident, and the fact that around 50 children were regularly attending the children's services in the portable hall, convinced Martha and David that there was a need for more suitable, larger premises for their work. With this in mind, they negotiated with the Local Council for use of the Public Hall.

The work expands initially in the Public Hall and later in the Village School. (1970-1977)
The work began in the Public Hall in October 1970 and continued there until March 1974, when the rent became too expensive for them to pay. Fortunately, the Village School became available, which they considered to be more suited to children's work. They moved to the school premises and were there until March 1977.

When they moved from their home to the Public Hall, numbers increased from twelve to around fifty, on average: this including boys as well as girls. Ages ranged from three to fifteen! *Children's Services* were held every Wednesday from October until March. A *Youth Club* was formed for those ages 10 and over.

Each year, the term was concluded with a *Parents' night* at the end of March (a SOIREE).

The kind of Soiree that David and Martha organised involved huge amounts of work and commitment from them, their helpers and the children involved. I will comment on such an occasion later. (These events bring back personal childhood memories for me, of a time when there were no televisions or video games; when children were asked to repeat a whole chapter of the bible, in the AV (easier to remember because of its rhythm) and for which they received a prize (the "Jack want-to-know" books, by Montague Goodman, spring to mind!) Children took part in "set pieces," holding up cards and often appropriately dressed up for the occasion.

David and Martha showed me an invoice for their Soiree held in March 1974 (dated 22/6/1974). It read:

180 bags (rolls, sandwich and cake) @ 14p		£25.20
85 (ice-creams)	@ 2.5p	2.12
Total		£27.32

The number of bags gives an indication of the large number of parents and children expected; while the ice-creams indicate the number of children, within the overall total.

Martha commented: *"It seemed that the whole village turned out on those occasions."*

Of particular significance during this period were:

Adult services held in the Public Hall
Martha recalls that, on one of four consecutive Sunday evenings, when the preacher at the adult services was *George Hanlon,*(whom I will refer to later) the oldest lady in the village accepted Jesus as her Saviour.

A second summer effort by the Lanarkshire Gospel Work (LGW) culminating in a very special "Sunday School Trip."

In the summer of 1974, the *LGW* again decided to hold their summer outreach effort, using their portable hall, in the field opposite the Kinnaird's home, with the full support of the local farmer and his wife.

The evangelist was the late *Denis Barnes* (supported by his wife *Hetty*) from Maddiston, Falkirk. During this period, they stayed with David and Martha.

Denis conducted adult and children's services and on Friday evenings they organised an Old Age Pensioners' (Senior Citizens') meeting. Martha said: *"The highlight of this was the pancakes made by Hetty!"*

The special event was a *Sunday School Trip,* which happened to replace the Chapelton Gala Day that year. This was held on Friday 28th June 1974, at *Lowberry farm*, in a field near Chapelton, on the left side of the road from Chapelton to Strathaven.

A large number of the villagers and children attended. *"This was a joyful occasion"* - reminiscent of less busy times, when such events, common in village communities at one time, brought local people closer together.

The outing involved games and sports for all ages - including football and rounders; races, fiercely contested! - Sack, three-legged, egg and spoon and straight races. These were followed by tea and orange juice in paper cups, and buns and cakes. *"With the sun shining (as always!); the smell of the fresh country air and the grass beneath their feet, a wonderful time was had by all."*

This was to be the fore-runner of similar events held in different venues in subsequent years. But more importantly for the Kinnaird's, it would help build up a rapport with the children and parents in the village, in the years ahead.

A new sun-lounge extension is built on to the Kinnaird's house, at 40 Shawton Road to accommodate the next phase of the Children's work (1977-1980).

The village school premises were only available for children's work on Wednesdays and from October through to March each year. The Kinnaird's wanted to extend the work to include Sundays and beyond the winter period permitted by the school. There was also growing pressure from the authorities to discontinue "after hours" use of the school premises.

They therefore decided to move the children's work to their own home, where the sun-lounge, which they had built, was able to accommodate up to 40 children. In this way, the work was extended to include Sundays as well as Wednesdays, all year round, in the friendly atmosphere of their home. This was a time of great blessing and the Kinnaird's were greatly encouraged by the nucleus of Christian helpers and encouragers in this phase of their work.

A group of children and workers in Martha & David's home. 103

*A final step of faith and a climax to their years of service for God, in Chapelton, realised in the erection of a new building, in Chapelton, at 30 Burn Road, Chapelton, "**Chapelton Evangelical Hall**" (1980-2004).*

Trustees and helpers

Greatly encouraged by the response of the village children and parents and faithful Christian helpers from different towns and villages in Lanarkshire, David and Martha became convinced that a new building, separate from their home, was needed if they were to expand the work among the children and youth in Chapelton; organise regular parents nights and adult services and meet with their growing band of helpers for times of prayer and bible study.

They shared this vision with other interested Christians and together they prayed about it. These prayer partners encouraged them to go forward, looking to God for guidance and, after careful consideration, and continuing practical advice and assistance from George Hanlon, in particular, on procedures and fund raising, they approached the relevant Local Authority. In 1979, the Council feued them the present ground for the new hall, for a period of 60 years, at a reasonable annual sum.

This was a courageous decision and an act of faith, as they embarked on their vision, believing that God would bless their efforts and that the necessary funds would be made available for the building and for future repairs and maintenance: that future period we now know, turned out to be more than 25 years! It also involved a huge continuing commitment and self-sacrifice on the part of David and Martha and the active trustees and helpers.

Their decision to proceed needs to be viewed against a background, at that time, and in the following years, of a rapid decline in adult attendance and membership in many assemblies and churches throughout the land. Sunday school work was also greatly diminishing and except for a few bright exceptions, children's work no longer thrived mid-week.

The problem would be exacerbated in the later years by Central Government legislation and in particular the *Child Protection Act* aimed at preventing child abuse but, which placed a significant administrative and financial burden on those seeking to undertake children's work. But the work in Chapelton was thriving and they pressed ahead!

Letters were sent out to Christian Brethren assemblies and interested individuals and a significant donation was also received from the *Laing Trust.*

God answered their prayers: the required finances were raised, as and when required and at no time did they have to borrow to meet the costs of the building operation.

David estimates that the cost of construction, excluding significant voluntary labour, was around £13,500, in the late 1970's. The building was fairly basic, with no frills but fully heated, with all the necessary amenities provided: the building warrant was granted. It was completed and ready for occupation in 1980.

But the work did not proceed without its trials and difficulties.

A solid core of helpers gathered round and the construction work was carried out but not without its problems. Assistance in the building was provided by the local council under a government aided scheme to encourage youths, who would otherwise be unemployed, to engage in building work under a supervisor. One of the requirements of the scheme was that accommodation would be provided for the youths who participated and George Hanlon kindly provided the use of his own caravan. Unfortunately, the scheme proved to be a disaster as the workers were undisciplined and the caravan was set on fire and completely destroyed.

In order to have the building work completed, the Kinnaird's provided the use of their garage, but this too was trashed and most hurtful to David and Martha was that their children too, were affected, when their bikes were vandalised. This was one of the most trying experiences the dedicated team had to endure during this period of the work in Chapelton.

Trustees were appointed and during the period of activity in the new building these included:

David Kinnaird
George Hanlon (East Kilbride) formerly Bothwell
Sam Reid (Hamilton)
Billy Fell (Douglas)
John Moore (Glassford) now deceased
David Smith (Glassford) now deceased.
Ian Purss (East Kilbride)

A number of the above were actively involved in assisting in the work, in various ways, on a continuing basis.

George Hanlon, who played a significant role in a number of ways, had been a missionary in Borneo, with his wife Phyllis for a number of years until he retired. It was a highlight, for us in the Shiloh Hall, in Glassford, when he came home on furlough to give us his missionary report.

Margaret Thomson, Hamilton, a talented musician provided the music on a portable organ at most of the services, including the choruses for the children.

Opening conference
When the building was completed and ready for the

services to begin, David invited the late *Willie Scott from Machermore*, in Newton Stewart, as the conference speaker. He accepted and the Conference was well attended. David had previously gone to help Willie during a number of summer months, prior to this invitation and Willie had been a source of inspiration to the Chapelton workers, during the building work and in the work they were now about to engage in.

Willie was a well-known and greatly respected figure in Christian Brethren assemblies throughout the country. He had, had built, and was then running, a Nursing Home at Machermore near Newton Stewart mainly for aged and infirm Assembly members. This was built and operated on *faith grounds*, depending on God alone to provide for the needs of the home through the gifts of assemblies and individuals.

The major aspect of their work in the new hall was again among children.

The Wednesday Club
This Club was organised for boys and girls of mixed ages.

The singing of bright, relevant choruses was a weekly feature of the meetings and was greatly enjoyed by the children.

Gifted children's speakers were invited, for the evenings. Most of them were or had been involved in children's work in their own locality and further afield and were well able to give relevant, illustrated Bible messages and often introduced new choruses. Names included Sam Reid (also a Trustee), who for many years carried out a children's work, in a deprived area, in Hamilton; Alistair Young (full time child evangelist) with painting skills and his well-known puppet, Jeremy; Gordon Anderson; Sam McMillan; Hugh Reid to name but a few, and latterly, I was able to help with my coloured over-heads, guitar and modern bible flannel graphs and occasional use of a very eastern looking puppet. (My wife Ann accompanied me to ensure the singing was "up to scratch".) Some of the above speakers also contributed to the Special Annual Events.

Prior to the building of the new hall, David had suffered an accident at work, which greatly affected his mobility and his health deteriorated during this period.

One of the Trustees suggested to Martha and David that they contact "Gospel Literature Outreach" (GLO) - a very successful international young people's outreach, with an established local centre in Motherwell. They did and an arrangement was made whereby one or two GLO students came regularly to assist with the work. The students were able to inject new ideas and introduce new choruses, which gave a significant boost to the work, while at the same time, the students gained practical experience working among children.

This arrangement lasted for many years and enabled the team to carry on this work with renewed vigour.

The Sunday School
Children's services were also held in the new building on Sundays. These were conducted by Martha with the help of Ina MacArthur and later Margaret Purss.

This work involved consecutive bible lessons, singing, quizzes and learning bible memory verses: some of the older girls also assisted.

Those who regularly helped in the Wednesdays and/or Sundays met for an annual dinner in the Kinnaird's home. It was also a popular venue after services were over, where the helpers enjoyed warm and happy fellowship together.

Sandy's choir for older girls
Shortly after the new hall was opened, a young man, who

lived in Strathaven, became a Christian at a holiday club in Leadhills. He came to Chapelton to offer help in the work there and seek encouragement on his Christian path.

While there, he started up a choir for the older girls and this choir went with Sandy and the Kinnaird's on Saturday nights, during winter to sing at "Tea Meetings." They even travelled as far as Kincardine, where Dennis and Hetty Barnes (referred to earlier in connection with the work in Chapelton) conducted an outreach work. Some of the girls' parents helped provide transport to those places and also attended the Tea Meetings.

For a number of years the choir also went carol singing in the Chapelton streets at Christmas time. This was a novel feature of their work among the children.

Martha recalls an interesting incident involving one of the choir girls whose family was moving from Chapelton to stay at a remote farm cottage between Dumfries and Annan.

The Kinnaird's were unfamiliar with the new area but, as the girl had become a Christian, they were concerned lest she lose touch with other Christians in her new area.

They managed to obtain the name of a Christian who lived in Annan and he informed them, that at that very time, a young Christian farmer, who lived some distance from Annan, had told him that he had a desire to assist in the Sunday School at Annan: this farmer *happened* to pass by the girl's family's farm cottage, on his way to Annan. He picked up the family of four each week and took them with him to the Sunday school.

The Kinnaird's arranged a small farewell party for her and she was presented with a *Bible and Text Picture*. They were sad to see her go. When they visited her later, they were surprised to discover that the cottage was "miles from anywhere." Surely the hand of God was in this convenient arrangement.

Lowberry Farm Trip (1)

The main Annual events associated with the children's work were:

The Summer Sunday School trip.
I have already referred earlier to the trip at Lowberry Farm. Others trips included, visits to Troon sea-front; Cumnock Park; Lanark Loch and Rouken Glen in Glasgow. These occasions were always well attended also by the children's parents.

Although careful steps were taken to ensure the children's safety, there was always the odd incident which gave cause for alarm. The Rouken Glen visit was one of those occasions recalled by Martha, but trips were seldom without their moments of anxiety. On this occasion, a small girl appeared to be missing and a frantic search was made for her. She

Lowberry Farm Trip (2)

was found shortly afterwards but, while the search was going on, two of the boys who were in the group started to fight, which added to the tension. None of the problems appeared to be serious and the leaders and children would retire at the end of the day, tired but happy.

The Christmas Service (Soiree)

Halloween was not an arranged night but, preparations had to be made by the Kinnaird's, for the many visits made on that evening by the children and others, who regularly attended their services. Theirs was an open house and they often had unexpected visits from children, who arrived to share a personal problem or happy event.

The *Soiree* was held just before Christmas, every year. The new building made it easier to prepare the children for this high-light evening.

More than half a century ago, the *Soiree* was a common event in many villages in Scotland but, the level of preparation by leaders and children in Chapelton was surely rarely repeated elsewhere during this period. The preparations necessitated many weeks of work in advance by Martha, her helpers and the children. A number of the *"pieces"* were produced by Martha herself.

Children of similar ages were each given a large card to hold up, in turn, with a letter of the alphabet clearly displayed on it. Prior to the event, the child had to learn by heart a number of rhyming lines, beginning with their own particular letter. As they stood in line, on the night, and each revealed the letter on their card and spoke their words by heart, the other children and parents who attended, watched as each letter was revealed to produce a word appropriate to the message which was being conveyed. Often the children dressed up, as the character they were chosen to represent. The children took their role very seriously and seldom needed prompting when repeating their lines. The parents, who attended, could at times be seen to apply a handkerchief to their eyes as they watched their own child – sometimes very young – make their very personal contribution to the message.

Today the advance of technology and pressures on time have made this feature precious and peculiar to those times, but what a binding effect it had on the village community.

The children often played musical instruments and sang carols and on one occasion, the Youth Club drew pictures to decorate the walls.

A large number of parents - often as many men as women - and children attended these Soirees.

The following week the children enjoyed their *Christmas Party*. Refreshments were provided and party games were organised for the children. The highlight of the evening was the appearance of "*Santa*" with his presents.

A group of workers and children taken after prizegiving.

Slow White and the Heaven Sorts - children taking part.

. . . and the aftermath (the washing in the Kinnaird's line).

For a number of years, the village council has invited David to become their *"village Santa,"* on Christmas Eve: a job which he clearly likes! He also plays Santa at the Play Group Party. Clearly, their work with children was valued and appreciated!

The Parents' night and Prize-giving, at the end of March.
Prize-giving was held yearly in March, bringing the previous year's work to an end. Again this event was well attended by parents and children.

A programme of events was organised for the evening, similar to the Christmas Service with choruses, a children's speaker and "pieces" by the children. The evening was concluded with the presentation of prizes, - usually a book or a Bible.

One year, the leaders decided to present a different programme for the evening. It was a musical drama based on the story of "Snow White", entitled *"Slow White and the Heaven Sorts"*. This entailed hiring costumes and a script. The children dressed up and sang and spoke their parts. It was well-attended and was an unforgettable night for the children.

Martha commented: *"You should have seen our washing-line for days after, with its many strange outfits hanging on it!"*

One final, one-off, event rounds off this part of their story:

Re-union for all the children, who had previously attended their services.
A date and venue was set for the reunion and invitations were prepared.

David and Martha had kept a record of all children who had regularly attended, over the years. There were over 500 children on the Register. The record contained names and addresses of the children, but by now many had moved house and some were now adults! Every effort was made to contact them.

The following example illustrates the efforts made to "follow up" and also indicates something of the blessings which resulted from the work among the children in Chapelton.

David visited the Library in Stonehouse hoping to find the present location of two former girls - Rhona and Lorna Gordon. The Librarian informed him that the family had relocated elsewhere but that she knew a friend who might be able to trace their whereabouts.

The librarian's friend followed up their enquiry and David received a 'phone call from Rhona, now grown up and living in Cumbernauld. She spoke with excitement in her voice and told him that she and her sister Lorna had become and

David and Martha at the re-union for all children who had attended the Children's services over the years.

were married to Christians. They came to the reunion and told the Kinnaird's that the children's services and contacts with Martha and David in Chapelton had been the first link in the chain leading them to accept Jesus as their Saviour.

Thrilled with this news, David later returned to the Stonehouse library to give the librarian a "thank-you" gift of a box of chocolates. To his surprise, he learned that the lady he had been in touch with regarding his request had only been in the library on duty, providing holiday cover, on that one occasion. Truly, "God's ways are past finding out".

Another girl, who had moved to Aberdeen, recalled the day she "gave her heart to the Lord" at the Kinnaird's children's services.

For the Kinnaird's and for many who attended the reunion that day, it brought back precious memories. Martha was reminded of the words of *Ecclesiastes Chapter 11 verse 1* *"Cast thy bread upon the waters: for thou shalt find it after many days."*

God has indeed been at work in Chapleton. May this be an encouragement to others to look to the Lord for blessing in their service and work among children.

**

Acknowledgements

1. While my main objective in this book is to show "God at work," against a background, which by its very nature involves major events in history, I make no claim to be a historian, nor do I present it as a history book: although after three years of thorough research, and cross-checking of data, where possible, I believe the historical background I have recorded is accurate.

I am indebted, in particular to the following for the *major sources* of material for the book:

(a) PART ONE - Early activities in Glassford and Chapelton.

Rev. William T. Stewart for kindly giving me freedom to use his invaluable book "*Glasford – the Kirk and the Kingdom.*" Had he not published it, the local record of events in Glassford, particularly during the period of the Druids, Covenanters and Quakers would have been lost in perpetuity.

- **Jim Frew, JP** compiled a record of "*The Church in Chapelton*" in a booklet, in which he included names of Chapelton people involved in Covenanter and Quaker problems etc. He greatly encouraged me in my initial efforts.

(b) PART TWO – The Jeanie Gilchrist story.

John Ritchie Ltd, Kilmarnock for permission to research and use the original material in the Book, on "*Jeanie Gilchrist*" (now out of date but written and printed by John Ritchie around 1910).

Rex Parry, author, of the **Historical map** (reproduced as my MAP 2) on "**Msiri's kingdom in 1880**", *in the Wikipedia free encyclopedia*, which sets out the historical background, at the time Jeanie Gilchrist and other missionaries mentioned in my book were active in Central Africa. I have used this map along with a modern map (MAP1) in my "Interlude and 2010 perspective on the Jeanie Gilchrist story". I am also indebted to **Wikipedia free encylopedia** for general information relating to this period.

(c) PART THREE – Kinnaird's Children's Work in Chapelton.

David & Martha Kinnaird, who co-operated with me in many meetings in their home, to enable me to produce this, the official record of this work.

2. Other sources of information include :

The Druids by Stuart Piggott,-Volume 63 in the series "Ancient Peoples and Places." - general background information on the Druids.

Financial Times and Luke Johnston, for permission to publish from Luke's column in the FT, his helpful summary on the remarkable impact of the Quakers on Britain's Industrial Revolution.

The New Statistical Account of Scotland (1845) Volume VI – Lanark, Parish of Glasford was prepared by the Rev. Gavin Lang, minister of Glasford Church of Scotland, at that time and he provided *inter alia* a full account of "*the sufferings of the people in the parish of Glasford*" *(*which included Chapelton), as originally recorded in the Parochial Registers, by the then minister *Rev. Francis Borland in 1692,* concerning the sufferings of the local people, in the 1660's. This information and much more has been incorporated into Rev. William Stewart's book and Jim Frew's referred to above and I have included some of the examples in this book.

Centenary of Hebron Hall Assembly, Larkhall, 1866-1966 by Alex Strang. Information on James Gilchrist and the Assembly in Chapelton.

Interlink and Echoes of Service. I have already acknowledged, in the book, help received from individuals in identifying names of places and their current modern equivalent, and important dates necessary to understand the story of *Jeanie Gilchrist*, and further up-dates to her story. In particular, I now acknowledge help in this regard and in other ways from **Interlink** (Scotland) and **Echoes of Service** (England).

"Selkirk Evangelical Church "40 years of Witness",church publication in respect of their connections with the *Arnot's and Jeanie Gilchrist.*

Ayrshire Post for permission to include the photograph and narrative relating to the visit of Jeanie Gilchrist's nephew, in 1956, to erect a permanent bronze plaque where she was buried.

3. John Ritchie Ltd, Kilmarnock, Publishers, for their support and agreement to publish this book.

4. Christian friends, including Trustees, of *the Chapelton Evangelical Hall,* who have supported me unstintingly in the production of this book.

5. Last, but not least my wife **Ann**, who has supported me during the three years of the gestation of this book, putting up with the litter of paper strewn throughout our home and the "occasional" (depending on from whose perspective!) 2 am's, as I struggled to process and record the book on my PC.